PICTURE PRAYERS

The Journey to
Picture Perfect Prayers

First published by O Books, 2009
O Books is an imprint of John Hunt Publishing Ltd., The Bothy, Deershot Lodge, Park Lane, Ropley,
Hants, SO24 0BE, UK
office1@o-books.net
www.o-books.net

Distribution in:

UK and Europe
Orca Book Services
orders@orcabookservices.co.uk
Tel: 01202 665432 Fax: 01202 666219
Int. code (44)

USA and Canada
NBN
custserv@nbnbooks.com
Tel: 1 800 462 6420 Fax: 1 800 338 4550

Australia and New Zealand
Brumby Books
sales@brumbybooks.com.au
Tel: 61 3 9761 5535 Fax: 61 3 9761 7095

Far East (offices in Singapore, Thailand,
Hong Kong, Taiwan)
Pansing Distribution Pte Ltd
kemal@pansing.com
Tel: 65 6319 9939 Fax: 65 6462 5761

South Africa
Alternative Books
altbook@peterhyde.co.za
Tel: 021 555 4027 Fax: 021 447 1430

Text copyright Heidi Hollis 2008

Design: Stuart Davies

ISBN: 978 1 84694 203 7

A CIP catalogue record for this book is available
from the British Library.

Printed by Digital Book Print

O Books operates a distinctive and ethical publishing philosophy in
all areas of its business, from its global network of authors to
production and worldwide distribution.
This book is produced on FSC certified stock, within ISO14001
standards. The printer plants sufficient trees each year through
the Woodland Trust to absorb the level of emitted carbon in
its production.

PICTURE PRAYERS

The Journey to
Picture Perfect Prayers

Heidi Hollis

BOOKS

Winchester, UK
Washington, USA

CONTENTS

Chapter 1   A Personal Prayer Perspective   1
Chapter 2   Importance of Prayer   7
Chapter 3   Poised for Prayer   15
Chapter 4   Placing Pictures in Prayers   23
Chapter 5   To Speak Like the Angels   31
Chapter 6   My Mind as a Guide   39
Chapter 7   God's Answers   47
Chapter 8   God's Visual Insight   53
Chapter 9   Practice in Pictures   59
Chapter 10   Photo Prayers   65
Chapter 11   The Dance of Prayers   71
Chapter 12   What's in the Air with Prayer   77
Chapter 13   Talking Strangers   83
Chapter 14   My Wireless Carrier   89
Chapter 15   God's Too Busy to Hear Me   95
Chapter 16   No Quotes: A Chapter of Prayers   101
Chapter 17   Essence of Time   105
Chapter 18   An Exercise in Prayer   113
Chapter 19   Analysis of a Life   119
Chapter 20   Responsibility   125

Other Books by Heidi Hollis:

Jesus Is No Joke: A true story of an unlikely witness who saw Jesus

To contact Heidi Hollis please visit:
www.HeidiHollis.com or www.PicturePrayers.com

Dedication
For Him, His Son and His Angels.

Acknowledgments

I would like to take this time and page to thank God for His Guidance and Jesus for His unwavering friendship and Sacrifice. I would also like to acknowledge the people involved in my life or those who have just passed me by on the street and say 'thanks' for teaching me their ingenious and lively tricks on getting by in this thing called Life! It is an existence that takes the right timing to know when to flourish, run, hide, laugh, jump, sit, gaze, wonder, be changed or be patient.

Now, balance is mine!

And for now, I will share part of a secret just as I promised to, since the beginning of "me".

Chapter 1

A Personal Prayer Perspective

Prayers have always been a big part of my life, but I am the first to admit that my form has been a bit flawed. From the moment prayers were presented to me as a small child, I knew it was not entertaining enough to keep my attention fully. All of this bowing of the head and keeping my eyes closed, proved to be too big of a challenge for a free spirited five year old.

I truly didn't have anything on my mind at that age, but to color with my crayons on paper and an occasional wall or two. My main focus at that age was to avoid getting busted by my mom with my beautiful wall murals of bunny rabbits and trees. So I was certain to draw low enough to make it look like my younger sister drew the bunnies instead of me. Truth be known, my tactics worked, unfortunately for my baby sis ☺.

Daydreaming of my next masterpiece was always on my mind, and being made to sit still in a church only got in the way of my drawing time. It was especially difficult when the pastor of my church would ask that everyone pray in unison, which for a kid only spelled out dire quietness. There was no rustling of papers, no fingering through the only book available in hope of spotting a rare drawing in there that might amuse me for a moment. Heads had to be bowed, eyes closed, fingers clasped, and by golly if you had a whistle in your nose, you had better learn to hold your breath!

When the moment came where the pastor called for this action of prayer, me and my siblings always looked at each other and braced for the worst. We always knew that one of us would not be able to hold our form and start giggling or screech our skirt wearing-bare thighs on the church pew. Then one of us would get a stern look from a nearby adult or even get a slight finger thumping from Dad if he even dared to sit for the sermon himself, which was rare.

The stress that was put toward these moments of praying in my church, made me grow weary, tired and absolutely petrified of messing up somehow. I began to associate praying with nothing more than some form of slow torture for children with no real purpose. I grew resentful for my time spent in prayer, and felt nothing "holy" or positive in being a part of a church sermon.

Sunday school gave me some relief, but still it was just more time for me to learn how to color inside of lines better. The only difference being that I had to color inside of some drawings of robed Biblical figures instead of my own freestyle of wall décor. There wasn't much else I could see that was of benefit for me to be in church or to even know what it was all about.

A couple of years later, at the age of seven, I went through an ordeal that no child should have to endure when my mother passed away in a car accident caused by her having a heart attack. Suddenly and harshly, I was met with having no warm arms of my mother to soothe or quiet me when I needed it. She was gone—but therein laid a mystery; where had she gone?

It was impossible for me to think that she had just left us with nothing to grasp or love. She couldn't and she wouldn't have done such a thing to me and my other eight siblings, half of which were already grownup but that still made no difference in their need for her. There was such desperation and searching in my heart to let her know how school went, to show her my latest drawing, or to have her stop my little sister from putting her finger an inch from my face exclaiming loudly, "I'm not touching you!"

There just had to be a way to reach out to my mom but for the life of me, at the age of seven, I was lost and empty.

One night, soon after my mother's passing, my sister Michelle came to my younger sister Keisha and me to talk to us about speaking with Mom. Michelle sat down on our shared bed and spoke quietly and asked, "Are you telling Mom you love her every night?"

I couldn't understand what Michelle meant because I didn't see Mom anywhere in the house to tell her that I loved her. Being literal as most children are at that age, I had the sense of getting up from the bed immediately to run around the house searching for my mom. I think I started nearing the edge of the bed to bolt out of the room when Michelle realized she needed to rethink what she was saying to her kid sisters who sat in front of her.

"I mean, are you praying to her each night before you go to bed?"

"Huh?" I felt like a toxic waste of disappointment poured over me when she mentioned that "sitting still in church practice" they liked to call prayer. I could see no reason for her bringing the topic up when it had nothing to do with Mom being near enough for me to say I loved her.

Michelle then started talking about the lessons we had learned in church and how God was in Heaven, but that we could talk to Him through our prayers. I remember sitting there puzzled and waiting for the link to Mom by talking about God. I already had a grudge against this God person to begin with for taking my mom! So I hardly cared to be talking to God anytime soon, being that one of the first things my father said to me after my mom died was, "I guess God needed her more than we did." Well, I was certain that nothing could have been further from the truth!

God had some explaining to do, I felt. With Michelle knowing full well about God having stolen our mother, I was perplexed why she was pleading His case before us. It was like watching an episode of *I Love Lucy*, where Lucy bungles a good thing and tries to explain why Ricky should still love her.

Luckily, Michelle was wise to the challenge in taking on a five and seven year old with stiff upper lips. Michelle managed to convince me enough to believe that I could at least send messages to Mom through my prayers with God. It seemed like a logical connection since He was responsible for her disappearance, right? So that night, Michelle knelt with me and Keisha for our first well thought out prayer.

In the middle of the prayer, however, Keisha and I interrupted to ask an important question. We wanted to know if it was okay to say hi to our dogs Buffy and Ling-Ling, too, since they also were presumed taken by God. Michelle gave us the okay to go ahead with the hellos, and helped us form a code of acknowledging Mom and the dogs. We took the oath that after each prayer we made that we had to talk with God and then give three blowing kisses toward the heavens for Mom and our beloved little Pekinese pooches.

For years, Mom, Buffy and Ling-Ling were put into my prayers each and every night like I promised, with my dedicated kisses and loving thoughts. My sister Keisha and I shared a room most of our childhood, and I often heard her sending off her prayers in the same manner I did. As years passed, the thoughts and needs of a young girl changed. Yet, out of pure habit the three kisses remained at the end of each prayer without any deep thought behind them.

It's odd to think that I was seven years old when I was taught that way to pray, but even stranger that I was nearly a teenager before I realized that I was still praying as I did as a small child. It was kind of funny that I had carried on giving kisses to my mom and dogs that had died so many years earlier. I, of course, didn't regret sending kisses to my mom, but two Pekinese dogs and one that passed the time by growling and nipping at us?

I couldn't fathom asking my kid sister if she was (and is) still praying with the kisses at the end, but I'm sure I'll know the answer to that soon enough. When I realized this repetitive kissing prayer flaw, I knew there were other methods of doing prayers even if it came to simply reciting them from the Bible. However, I felt that I still got my main objectives across in asking for blessings, forgiveness, taking care of my family, and then "smooch, smooch, smooch—blow"! I even held the proper form together with my hands together and my eyes closed. Everything had been approved by the "powers that be" and Michelle, so at the time I saw no necessary need to try and interject change in my prayers.

There was nothing fancy or exaggerated about my prayers either. It was, "God bless this, that and the other thing, and even the sibling I fight with all the time. I saw a kid on television with no food who needs help, I have a class exam that I haven't studied for, and please give me guidance on making the right decisions. Amen."

As I grew up through my teens and into my early adult years, I did begin to take more solace in having a better understanding that there actually was a God. It even sank into my head that this God actually listened to prayers, that is; after I got the distinct impression that when in need the most, my prayers were being answered. Some of the answers I got were so apparent, that I could hardly get them out of my mouth before something occurred which made the prayer request unnecessary.

I wasn't a rocket scientist, but I managed to put two-and-two together to see that this all added up to some higher power being in attendance. I felt then that it was a good thing that I was at least taught how to keep in touch with this power called God. For me, the more little miracles of answers that came forward, the more I felt I needed to keep committed to praying and interject more heart and vigor into them.

Of course, being on the receiving end of getting answers wasn't all I sought or cared about. I found it comforting to know that there was a Creator that cared about my dilemmas in life. It was like having a best friend that never left my side, and never had any ulterior motive for being there for me. God was just there, because loving is what He was about and putting a false front forward just seemed unfathomable.

Heck, I liked what I'd heard about this God guy (for the most part), and truly felt I couldn't go wrong in having some faith in what I was taught about Him. But darn it all, praying just was not my most favorite thing to do! I think somehow I would revert to my "sitting quietly" in church torture, when I thought about praying. I wanted to talk to God, of course, but having to perform it as I was taught and to pray so seemingly perfect, just continually made me dread it.

I had always hoped for a better way to pray, but I never truly thought that there was a different way, nor did I ever aim to search out a different form of prayer. Yet, somehow, praying got rerouted in my life and ultimately transformed me. There was so much I didn't know, and so much that needed to be shared.

Now, in fact, is my sharing time.

If there's any topic in the history of man that's needed a refresher course, praying should be near the top of that list. Yes, I know the saying, "if it isn't broke, don't fix it." Truth be told, at least for me, something didn't exactly flow right about my praying and I had no clue on how to make it any better. Lucky for me, I later learned how to blow the dust off from my mental prayer book to help start from the point I left off. One deep breath, blow, and suddenly I saw the title of my prayers more clearly.

Who knew?

Chapter 2

Importance of Prayer

Whenever I look at a topic of meaning related to me, I feel that there's always got to be some foundation laid down before I can see what a pretty house can be built or at least make some renovations to it. In being a visual person and someone with less than average patience to find answers to riddles, I looked at the subject of prayers from the shingles of my imaginary "topic house" and worked my way down. Just the opposite manner in which would be expected, which is typical "me" again.

Before I had my grand revelation and guidance on how to incorporate better prayer tactics into my life (yes—I have to bore you with the details), I went through a lot of awkward stages in examining my prayer habits. In becoming a more conscience minded, human being while growing up, I began to form my own opinions about issues in my young life. I realized I didn't like bullies (especially ones in the playground), putting ants in the freezer only to revive them later wasn't a kind experiment (they did usually wake up though depending on their length of time of deep freeze), kids with different abilities weren't to be made fun of (I was nearly considered one of them at one time—so it was easy to see that it wasn't cool to make fun), putting turtles, rocks, fish and dirt in the bathtub of my parent's newly built home isn't smiled upon (however, it was laughed about by at least one of my parents—I won't even mention the reaction of the other), and I eventually accepted that my manner of praying and the content of my prayers—in general—sucked (this feeling came and went at times)!

Yes, I know I have already alluded to, complained about, dropped a bomb on, and even whined a bit about how I didn't like how I felt about the mere act of prayer. Yes, I know I've already said that I knew I needed prayer in my life and in my soul I could actually feel that it was necessary and even helpful. Yet, somewhere, somehow I began to feel that something just wasn't right when it came to my praying. So I started thinking in the backwards fashion that I tend to visit from time-to-time, to a fuzzy place where I now believe I have my own reserved parking space for what I call "doubt" and think of things like: "If such an act like prayer was so important but I wasn't dedicating myself fully in the right way, then I felt I must have struck upon something even more confusing. Maybe my inner self was trying to tell me that I was wrong all along, that perhaps prayer just wasn't so important!"

Now how weird a conclusion was that? And I knew it.

So, there was no question that I needed to get to the tangled root of my dilemma, so I looked deep into what I felt about prayer. As it seems with most outcomes in life, childhood experiences and lessons were part of the culprit as I have mentioned I knew to be part of my personal resistance to praying. Yet, whenever I heard the word "prayer" I would indeed automatically think of it as a way of speaking to a positive, higher power. So, I knew that in order to rectify my feelings, that I had to detach the particles left in me from childhood on the practice of prayer being connected with my noted anxiety.

How odd it was for me to think that here I had, in some form, held onto being made to sit still in church for prayer as part of my prayer-conscience self. I disliked prayer because I was made to, something I promised to do with my sisters, and then on top of it, here I was praying to the Man above who took my mother away! Well, it was no wonder why I disliked prayer with all of that looming in my head. I think I was around the ripe age of twelve when I thought on all of these above mentioned aspects of my prayer distaste. Heck, who I am kidding? I knew I just loathed the simple act of praying at that age, but I at least considered my reasons why. I suppose I thought too much as a kid ☺.

Luckily, I continued to pray after my twelve year old ponderings whether I liked it or not, and pray I did. My prayers were filled full of sheer positives and aimlessness all at the same time. In all honesty, I think sometimes that I continued to speak to God year after year while growing up, night after night, out of pure feelings of duty and then out of habit. It was just something I did, that prayer thing. Then there were those times that it was absolutely awesome to have this invisible force connect with me where I felt something loved me no matter what.

Yeah, praying was no friend, but at times it was my only friend.

Sometimes I got angry at it, and grew resentful that it was needing to be addressed when I was at my most tired time before going to bed at night. It was always an errand that had to be done, and sent out to what I thought at times was just a void. That is, until I actually sent it out and had an inkling that my prayer hit home to some force.

What was this praying? Why did it disturb me, and yet make me feel so darn complete to even know that I was doing it? My inner self was trying to tell me something. It was saying that I needed prayer, and prayer needed me. So, I finally agreed that I would just accept this praying aspect into my life and not argue as much in my head when it needed to be done.

It wasn't long before I ventured off into another nagging aspect of prayer. I had to be nearly fifteen when I thought to drill a few holes into the frozen tundra (which was located not too far from Lambeau Field—Go Packers) called my head, and think bigger than just me and my prayer struggle. "Open-mindedness," yes, that's the word I'm looking for and that's what I welcomed into my head holes.

I began to slowly allow more acceptance and reasoning to be applied to why prayer existed in the first place, and why it was asked of me and everyone else on this planet. So I wandered on into those thoughts more and explored the vast world of prayers where I learned a wealth of knowledge and found more acceptances in myself. Thus began my journey into a whole new curiosity within myself, prayer and my need to reach out to God.

I knew that in some people's faiths that they were taught to pray to God, and some even directed their prayers to others. Even I admitted to having prayed to my dead dogs as a young kid, or at least acknowledged them to say "hi". So I could hardly knock someone for what drove them to believe as they did, even if I personally feel I'm aiming my prayers in the best direction. I was taught that it was important to speak to God Himself, so He could guide, bless and protect me and others around me.

When I think about these notions today, I still don't know any better points to be made. Sure there are sometimes bits and extras to be thrown in the mix on occasion, but the meat of my soup dishing to God remained to be about the same to ask for His help in all matters. It became my way of relaying to God, in at least some form.

Then I got to rationalizing my reasons for prayer even more when I thought how else am I to get closer to God if I were not on speaking terms with Him? I doubted that isolating myself to avoid sinning would work, or bungee jumping to feel free (unless the chord broke) would make the cut either. I have seen some odd routes taken to reach God, but nothing seemed more pure and revealing than just a little soul juice poured into a tall glass of prayer.

Without praying, there is a lot less linking up going on from my end of the stick. As I understand it today, God is always thoughtful for His creations and is tending them religiously, meaning He sees us and all of His creations on a routine basis. So then, if God makes an effort to help out in my life, that's some form of communication from His end. He's reaching out toward me to make an effort to show He's got me on His mind.

Now then, if I sat here on my backside and hardly gave a wink God's way, I can only guess what that tells Him. It'd probably spell out that I hardly regard His existence, for one. I'd also gather that God would think that I didn't see Him as being very important. So I truly don't see how I could show that I acknowledge His existence without saying anything to Him every now and then.

It's so apparent to me now that if I don't pray to God, I might as well turn my back to God, which is essentially the same thing. Even if I have a good friend, and stop calling them, that friend will get the idea that I don't care about them anymore. Same with God, if God isn't seen as important enough to even say "hi" to, my guess is that He's not very happy about it and it may even be a bit depressing for Him—for all I know.

At this point in my life I can't help but to wonder if people do not keep up their communication with God, if that would then be welcoming the opposite of God. There aren't many people that I know who are overly anxious to have rotten things come into their lives or happen to them. Yet, even I can see when I turn the light off in my bedroom at night, that all I see around me is darkness.

Turning off the light connection to God feels to be pretty much the same to me. Of course, a welcoming mat wasn't put out in hopes that negativity would engulf a person just because they slack in the prayer department. But a "Do Not Disturb" sign wasn't hanging on the door either.

I believe a clear message can be posted to the darker things in this life, if it's apparent and known where a person stands in God's light. It's almost common sense to me now that communication with God is essential, that is, if I care about my very well being. Yet, I'm adamant that praying shouldn't be a forced thing or done for the wrong reasons either, but instead reflect a part of who a person is.

If I were to go into prayer *just* to show obedience to God—that just doesn't seem right for some reason (although I think with my childhood prayer oath I kind of took it that way). Saying a prayer *only* to be forgiven for something, just feels to fall short, as well. I can think of a ton of things that wouldn't vibe right for me or anyone to pray solely about, but do I dare list some of them here?

Yes, I think I dare-th ☺.

Let's see, there's praying that ones spouse gets picked up by aliens and is never heard from again so you can get their life insurance (wrong and supernaturally cruel)! There's praying for God to forgive you for lying to someone, only to lie and lie again, never changing your ways (white-lies can count too). There's praying that you don't get caught cheating on your spouse under any circumstance, when your cheating isn't something you should have done in the first place and forget to ask for forgiveness for that act alone (big no-no)! Oh, the list doth travel on!

Going into prayer for reasons that are fully self-centered or selfish, just touches the wrong heartstrings for me, but I think everyone is guilty at some point in doing that. I know I have those days where everything seems to go wrong and I just plop it all God's way and I forget to ask for anyone else to get a blessing squeezed in there. It's nice to know that God understands how that happens, just as long as I don't make a habit out of doing that sort of praying, and then even I won't feel guilty about it.

I think I'm the Queen of Guilt when it comes to praying, and I'm glad I've learned to give myself a little slack. Learning to forgive myself for being human, I feel, is a huge step in learning under God's watchful eyes. If anyone would know how tough it is to get things right or to at least keep trying, the Creator of this creation would know. He planned it all to go this way, and no other way. Change it, and then it's not God's work.

But there is an issue along this topic that creeps into my mind, where I can argue the point of either side on the intention in prayer: If I am to go into prayer, and my whole heart isn't leaning in one direction for change, forgiveness and blessings; God just might get a clue and take note of my reluctance. I mean really, if I'm holding back a part of me to keep on doing the same mistake continually, will this "half of an effort prayer" be as effective?

I mean, of course I don't think that the effort should be dropped if me or anyone else isn't able to go whole heartedly into prayer, but I think it's important to show there's a difference on the weight of a prayer if I give God *all* of me. The cool thing about God and prayer is, though, I can show the good and the reluctant parts of me that don't want to change, and He'll have a look at it and help inspire change.

Come to think of it, I don't recall anything in the Bible saying I can only come to God in prayer if I am fully able to change. Being *willing* to change would help the matter, of course, but there's no absolute prerequisite for anyone going into prayer. Praying is available for everyone, there's no stern looking fellow standing at the door to judge people to open up the gates to prayer. It's just you and your heart, sitting there quietly with the keys to connect.

Ah, that thought brings me back to my imaginary "topic house" with the shingles on the rooftop. Some homes are built firmly with a strong foundation and then there's framing, and sometimes brick to secure the interior from the outdoor elements. Some homes even have a natural fireplace to help keep things cozy and create a nice little gathering place, much like the heart of a home.

The fire that burns in the fireplace often spurn conversation, laughter and special moments, which I'm suspicious gathers into the warm flames and pipes through the heart of the home through the chimney. But for homes without a heart of fire, there is no chimney, so the shingles on the roof remain uniform with no breaks for the heart of fire to share what takes place in the home.

On the outside, the home may look lovely and strong. But without a way of sharing what makes the house a home by not allowing the heart of the home to vent, those living in the house might suffocate.

A long analogy for a simple reason, I believe that some people don't realize that they need to vent who they are and share that with someone who will always listen. Speaking with God is not only an option; it's a necessity if His creations are to thrive. Appearances and ones style of prayer shouldn't matter, just as the outside of a home doesn't. Allowing oneself to express openly and grow with God in all ways positive is all that should be of concern.

Chapter 3

Poised for Prayer

Bent knees, sharp focus, a good memory and folded hands; these used to be the thoughts that came into my mind when I thought of those who prayed and prayed well. The pastor at the church I grew up in held his poise tightly, and the man never missed a beat or even tripped as he walked with his eyes squinted closed. If he wasn't quoting a prayer—by memory—from the Bible, he had a freestyle of prayer that could knock your socks off!

He didn't seem to forget to leave out anyone, anything or any poor soul in the world who needed prayer at that moment in time, either. It was: "God bless the cataclysmic events in blah, the needy people in blah, Mrs. Shoe who lost her blah, and the tiny dust mite who tripped and sprained its blah."

All I could think of was, "Man, he's good!" Sadly enough, I almost capitalized "he's" just now, that's how good I thought he was!

In trying to be a dedicated person to God as a young girl (from time to time anyhow), I felt that I'd never get to the level of this man in front of me with his kind of tongue for prayer. For one, I didn't have the capacity to even think as large as the world as this man did, and I surely couldn't have the nerve to share what my prayer might sound like in front of all of those people! Who really has the nerve to do all of that?

As an adult, I now realize that this pastor and others like him have gone through a lot of training and practice to be able to do what they do in such a seemingly flawless fashion. Being a kid, it wasn't explained to me that this guy had the flow that he did because of his background but I think it would have helped to know so I wouldn't feel the pressure to think that I had to be that good. How strange it is to think that prayer can be held as a spectacle of some sort. But truly, it seems that from the beginning of prayer as a concept that there has often been someone who led a congregation or gathering of people into prayer.

Out of the tradition of the Christian Bible, there are often times a centerpiece person who talks about God, and teaches us other folks how to be closer to God. Those centerpieces from the Bible get their names written down, and have retained a ton of respect over the centuries still till this day. Whether it's realized or not, I think we all in some form look up to our spiritual leaders, and use them as a human example of what we should strive to be.

It's not anyone's fault that we don't all aim to inform ourselves about the practice that goes into being a spiritual leader in today's world. Yet, from my uninformed perspective, it sure would have helped me to be somewhat in the "know" so I wouldn't feel that I fell short in my prayers, so much of the time. I even tried different approaches to get myself and my prayers up to par to something resembling what I'd witnessed in church, yet something always seemed to make me feel insufficient. There were a lot of aspects to consider that went into prayer, and I wanted to understand it all.

First there was the poise of prayer, which was all I was ever taught to belong to the art of praying. There is the head bowing, where you have to keep your head loyally down to show respect to whom you are speaking to. It reminds me of those who approached the kings of old, where everyone was expected to bow before their ruler of the day. No doubt then God should receive such a respect, if not more.

The eyes are then closed tightly for prayer, which I am guessing helps to keep one's focus so as not to be distracted by what is before you like your dirty shoes or crumbs on your lap, since your head is already down. Come to think of it, there was a tendency to show humility to someone who is superior to yourself back in the day where you would not dare look him or her in the eye. As if to come as only but a servant to one's master, you would not dare approach to ask a favor while standing eye-to-eye with your master. With God being the Master over all of us, it sounds like a good idea so as not to insult Him if we come to Him to serve and worship Him.

Then of course there's the hands being brought together where fingers may be clasped, which should be done before closing ones eyes if you have poor right and left hand coordination. Personally, I can't think of a reason off the top of my head why putting one's hands together was introduced into prayer. If one's hands were bound as a servant, begging for mercy from their master, it would resemble such a pose. Either way, I think that's one issue for me to type into a search engine to see where any of this came from.

Anyhow, as a kid (and as an adult) I did all of the above, and even sometimes did the "bent knee praying" which always was a bit painful with my boney kneecaps. So I usually tended to pray while lying in bed at night, already under my covers all snug and cozy. I'd usually get to the part about protecting my parents, watching over my siblings, and that's about all I could cover. Before I'd know it, that one element of prayer in closing of the eyes was a bad combination with already being comfortable in bed. I'd fall asleep so fast and hard after starting my prayers, it wasn't even cute or funny!

Yet, my intentions were always so strong to keep loyal to my prayers that after an undefined amount of time, I'd awake in horror that I didn't put the finishing touches on my prayer. So I'd search my mind on where I was at, then thinking I'd cover all my bases I'd pass the question in God's direction to make sure I mentioned this or that and would say the magic words, "In Jesus' name, Amen."

When I say I awoke in a panic, even as a kid, I am not kidding! It was so ingrained in me that I had to get those prayers in and in such a way, that I felt my prayers were only at half-staff on the flag waving scale of importance if it wasn't done properly. Especially being, I was also still saying hello to my mom and dogs in Heaven, and I'd hate to disappoint them.

I took it all so seriously, not only due to what my sister Michelle taught me, but from what my church instructed me, as well. I was so rigid in my praying where it was all so routine—that is, unless I had to pray for more calm in regard to a bullying sibling of mine who liked to sit on me or steal my candy as a hobby—so my need for patience changed priority in being able to breathe or eat! I knew then, as I know now, that most of my praying was coming from my head more than my heart. All of that straining myself physically to try and stay conscious even, or by doing the bent knee praying, nothing seemed to add any more deep dedication on my part.

Yet, as mentioned earlier, I rationalized that prayer was essential, so I kept up with whatever it was I had and I never forgot to at least try. I had always hoped there was an easier and better way, but to say better is almost not fair for those who truly enjoy the manner in which they pray. So I'll have to say that I'd hoped that there was a different way that I could express myself to God, without feeling that I didn't give of who I am to Him.

Without purposely aiming for another way of praying, God saw to it that I could have some relief in feeling complete in speaking with Him. Who knew it would amount to my sharing what was taught to me, to be taught to others to help ease their minds, as well.

I can at least be hopeful that my experience will alleviate some praying fears out there. Hmmm, now the word "fear" doth strike a chord in me; where did that come from? One would think that word wouldn't come into play in a book on such a positive topic, where I was about to end this chapter when there it popped out (yep—it was going to be a short chapter)!

You know, just when you think you know yourself and why you think and feel the way you do, you sit down to write a book and then you discover you didn't know as much as you thought you knew about yourself! That, or I'm half nuts ☺. I literally just recalled the outright fear that I had in praying as a child (even into adulthood). I mean, I was taught that God was a fierce and punishing God who rewarded those who did as they were told and were faithful.

It was kind of hard to swallow that I was to be praying to a God who could and would slice me in half if I dared to stray from Him. Then to think that I had to pray to Him and love Him, and be pure about it? Yipes!

I feared praying to my core!

I mean, not all of the time, of course. I didn't think about all of the ramifications of praying and why and how and who was going to get me if I didn't do it well enough. But I know now that I did indeed have some fear in me about performing well in my poise of prayer. There was even some nervousness involved, because I didn't want to curtsy wrong or offend God either.

Imagine a jester in the court of a brutal yet glorious king back in some ancient historical castle that I can't even name because it was so great (or I just can't think of any at the moment). This king has the reputation of knighting only a select few of those loyal to him and his reign, and all others were considered suspect until they could prove worthy. Being on the outside of this king's courtly trusted knights also left you vulnerable to beheadings, and no one was anxious for that community entertainment to happen to themselves!

Then there's the court jester. He's not exactly a trusted member of the king's court, and he's not an outsider either. There's this fine balance of where the jester's place is, and he does his best to keep the king impressed with his loyalty and dedication to keep the king happy with his performances. But the jester knows what the king is capable of in being able to destroy him with one wave of his scepter to order his demise. The jester does truly like the king and keeping him happy, but the jester cannot help but to fear if he doesn't please the king at every turn he might be the next social event.

Oh, the fear of the jester! I think I had a bit of the jester bug in me!

I wanted God to be pleased by what I did and how I regarded Him, but I also knew and was taught that God was a punisher of wrongdoers. Yes, and I knew that God forgave, too. Yet, it was too hard to put it all in my head to register how He could do such horrible things (although considered done to those who were deserving) and yet be so sweet and peaceful. It's like saying there's this vigilante down the street who will kill all jaywalkers, but he'll make you an awesome apple pie if you cross the street at the corner and ask nicely!

To offend anyone on their view of God is not my goal, but in the mind of a child (and even adults), aren't we all a bit imaginative on what is meant by subjects presented to us?

There was such a raw fear at times when it came to the idea of whether I was pleasing God and speaking to Him purely for the right reasons. God knew my heart, knew my reasons and everything before I would even come to Him, so why come then? I would only feel nervous that I was doing something wrong, more especially as I was maturing and realizing I was passing the "years of innocence" retained for the young in God's court of justice.

So yep—doing good by God, was a fear and I still didn't want to go to Him for the wrong reasons for sure. Now I admit that I had it all wrong in being afraid of God, but I didn't much appreciate being told about consequences to encourage me to speak to God and be faithful to Him. I feel it's already in us to know God as a friend who is only overprotective of His flock to be sure that no one taints or harms them.

Just as we would lay down our lives to protect those that we love, God would do the same. If someone were outside our home, threatening to harm or influence our loved ones to lose their very souls, that's when our boxing gloves come on! A discussion might ensue where you would try and talk the perpetrator out of their plot or unknowing and clumsy misconceptions of what they were doing and why. But if the stranger persisted, there may be only one choice but to end their attempts by any means necessary.

God would do no less.

I know this now and have no fear about speaking with Him in any manner that is respectful. I don't feel He will destroy me on the spot now for not crossing all of my "t's" and dotting my "i's". I have found true freedom in my love for God and speaking to and with Him, just as it should be and feel.

Chapter 4

Placing Pictures in Prayers

Recently, I've pinched myself to make sure that I am no different than the next person. Not that there was anything scientifically specific about the pinch, just the usual quick squeezing between the thumb and index finger. Results now show that I am, thus far, human and flawed.

I have seen some odd things in my life, things that are unexpected, weird, and even downright holy things. In the case of my learning to pray anew, I can only refer to it as a life changing and holy experience.

To think that I could even for one second imagine all that occurred, gives me way more credit for being a genius; a title I surely don't own or carry on a sash on this body! I therefore give full credit and thanks to God for even allowing me a glimpse to personally better my communication skills with Him. If what I've learned even helps another person one iota of a bit in their prayers, then hot-diggity-dog, it was all worth it!

In April 2000, I was attending an intriguing conference full of friends, laughter and lots of good conversation. Whenever I get around good and intriguing people, my energy levels rise. This element in turn meant that I would be met with little sleep for this weekend event, with so much positive energy running amuck. I wasn't the only one at this conference who lost track of time and sleep. A friend of mine at the time I'll just call Josiah (not his real name), also kept the same pace I did while we were there that year. We both came to the conference with a large group of other friends who just couldn't handle the all night hours that we both seemed to manage.

After a whole night of deep conversation and meeting more and more interesting visitors to this conference intended for deep thinkers, Josiah and myself finally thought it to be a good idea to actually sleep. It was sometime in the early afternoon when we decided to head back to our multi-shared hotel room for some much needed "Zzz's". Our other traveling friends had already slept and gone, so the room was empty for us to completely lay our exhausted bodies on our own beds across from each other.

There was no putting on my pajamas, or fluffing up my bed or pillow, it was just me and my dead weight against that bedding. All I remember is flattening my head against the pillow and checking out of this universe, for all I cared at the time. I felt like I had barely laid my limp body down for five minutes before something noticeably incredible started to happen to me.

I awoke, in some sense of the word or in another state, in a mist of white and crystal blue light. Soon afterwards, the mist began to slowly clear where I was able to start to see forms and figures. I saw people sitting or kneeling solemnly, with their heads bowed, their eyes closed and fingers clasped or placed together. Others just had their heads bowed with their hands flat on their laps, or were looking up toward the sky with tears in their eyes. These people were scattered around me in all directions in different scenes and environments of their own. It became clear to me that the people I was seeing were praying. Some of these people were alone in prayer while others sat near another in what looked like an effort of prayers.

I could see some of these various people's lips moving, as if to mumble words of their prayers into faint whispers. I could sense and see that these people were truly arranging their words in the best form they knew how to send God's way to ask what was needed of Him. Yet, from where I was, I couldn't hear their outright words. Then as if a trail left these people's lips, their words started to dance out in front of me in a form of energy.

The words took on a different life of their own and started to transform into scattered images. The people, who these words came from, then started to fade away out of my view. Yet, their converted words into these images remained and loomed in the air before me. To say exactly in detail what these visuals entailed, I cannot recall, and I'm certain I was not meant to describe them. Peculiarly enough, these images I saw were incomplete where they had pieces missing or parts that floated way off to one side of my view in a jumble of other pieces. Many of these images even lacked luster and color, while some only had certain parts of the image highlighted with special emphasis. Some of the images were even hard to view as if they were out of focus or had less energy connected to them as the other images did.

The images remained in midair when I began to realize, that somehow or another I was in the middle of knowing and seeing the energy of prayers. How and why I was there, came to mind and then left me quickly as a part of my soul slowly awakened. An urge or instinct came to me to try and make sense of these jumbled puzzle pieces of images. The words that first created these images were no longer a part of what was in front of me; only the intentions were felt to remain.

I remember standing before each image trying to get a sense of what was meant, and it wasn't as if I could gather exact details of what the prayer words were. I would have felt like an eaves-dropper had I been able to hear verbatim what was only intended for God. That would not be my place, of course.

Instead, what I experienced while standing in front of these prayers was more like a vibe of meaning. Just as I can see when waves are uniform and unbroken on the surface of an open body of water, the vibe could be felt in this form. Although, these "waves" in front of me did not feel complete, as if some of its strength was lost from some unseen wave breaker.

After some intense moments, one by one, I was able to gather the deeper vibe of each prayer in front of me. It took some effort to lean in and look for some color, or to see the other parts of the picture materialize through some form of encouragement. It was hard to comprehend why, what seemed like such a simple meaning, took so much effort.

With the task in front of me completed, my mind began to wonder again about why I was there. Then suddenly the scene changed and the solved prayer puzzles vanished. Soon to follow, a life of visuals came into view.

My sight was filled with movement, as if I were watching a movie that indicated the lives of us all. In this "life movie" vision I saw homes, grass, bikes, bills, homework, relationships, love, pain, toys, cars and all kinds of people who ever met other people. Just as quickly as the life movie was played, several parts of this movie were cut directly out of the scenes as it was still being played without any part of the life movie being left blank. Much like right-clicking and pressing "copy" instead of "cut" to move and save an image on a computer.

The copied pictures from the scenes were then assembled in front of me to the left side of my view. Then I felt love and feelings of concern come forward directly from the portion of the scenes where the copied pictures were taken from the life movie. The energy of these emotions then moved to the opposite side, to my right, from where the cut pictures were in my view and hung there for a moment like glistening stars.

The next thing that happened I only have one way of explaining what it looked and felt like (it reminded me of slapping some glue on the back of a photo to create a sure thing to have the photo stick where you wanted it): the feelings of intention floating before me, sucked into the images and blended as if they had never been apart.

There was an overwhelming feeling of oneness that came over me, the images and intentions were completed and truly; *one*. I marveled at each of the images as if they were each a fine artwork in their own right as they each teemed with such solidarity. There was such poise, beauty, and an absolute strength of clarity to what I was viewing.

Then one by one, each of the images converted into a spinning ball of beautiful light. They each paused only for a moment as if to allow me one last look. Then with tremendous speed, each ball of light quickly shot straight past me into a vast space and then upward where they went out of view. There was no doubt in my heart that each sphere of light was then headed on their way to the one they were truly destined for, God.

After marveling at the departure of these spheres, this lesson without words changed once again. I felt I was being guided to practice this lesson in my own life. If I could give words to the intentions that were being directed my way, this unseen guidance was saying, "Take what you see in your own life, envision it and put your feelings to what you have concerns about."

It was such a clear feeling of request, so I put into action what I had just seen and took my turn. I paused for a moment to think of a moment or concern I had. I then thought of my parents, having lost my mother at a young age I always dreaded the thought of anything happening to my father or stepmother. So I hoped that my folks would be happy and healthy for many years to come. I was also always concerned that I was making the right choices on my spiritual path, so I put the intention to mind that I'd hoped I was making good decisions in that manner.

I looked around for a visual in my head of my parents going about their daily lives and then thought up one of myself sitting in deep thought. I then steadied my visual camera and took a snapshot to capture those images in my mind. I got out my mental glue and then swabbed a bit of my intentions of concerns on the back of each snapshot. With my prayer package in hand, I then focused God's way and sent my delivery to Him with my usual, "In Jesus' name. Amen."

I had closed my eyes to focus myself for this prayer and opened them just in time to see my spheres of light shoot off towards God. I was amazed at how fast and easy it was for me to formulate my prayer and to feel satisfied with its content.

I had heard no direct words up to this point during this lesson, when I was met with what truly seemed to be outright words. Being in the state that I was, and with all of the emotions coming forward in me and at me, for these intentions to stand out as they have in my mind leads me to feel these were more direct expressions. Whether by direct words or not, these intentions were floated my way directly as if to be sure I got the message straight.

"Words fall short of what is meant." Then another image of a person's life came forward with their feelings attached to it: "Prayer can be done this quickly, this is how we communicate."

Then the acknowledgment was put in place that people needed to know and learn this lesson that was presented to me. I felt the indescribable urgency of this matter from this seemingly faceless force surrounding me with love and gentle guidance. I say "seemingly faceless" only because I saw no distinct face or image of a person. I instead felt the familiarity of what and who surrounded me. It felt like the voices of angels who I believe shadow us every day to help see to it that we are safe.

When the presence said, "This is how *we* communicate" I had connected that it meant this is how they spoke with each other and how they spoke to God. They, being the angelic protectors of God's creation of man. I felt a true connection and honor for what they had shared. When it was presented how others needed to know this information, I made a silent promise that I would share what they had shown me.

The image then faded, as the agreement and lesson felt in place and complete. Soon afterwards, I bolted up in my bed after what felt to be close to an hour of so-called "sleep". I was so excited about what I had just seen and learned that I sat right up and quickly told Josiah about my experience. It was odd to think of how after so little sleep, Josiah and I were absolutely still mentally focused and crisp.

After I rambled on about what I'd seen, Josiah seemed moved and calm as he laid back in bed with a wondering thought saying, "Well that makes sense!" I then rolled back onto my own bed and agreed saying, "Yeah, it does. I wonder why no one has ever thought of it before."

I knew that I hadn't, and didn't think of it on my own. There is a time and a place for everything, and it certainly seemed that God had His reasons to share this with me. Now I felt it was my turn to hold up my end of the agreement to share what I learned, including how and all of the in-betweens.

Chapter 5

To Speak Like the Angels

Well, that's what it seemed to be to me, anyhow.

An angel's way of talking had to be different from our own way of communication, but I never really thought of it before. When looking at the stories from the Bible, and how angels communicated to people, I knew that they did it in various ways. Sometimes they spoke outright to witnesses as they did when the stone was rolled away from Jesus' tomb. The angel there told Mary Magdalene, Mary mother of James and Salome, that Jesus had risen and wasn't there any longer. Other times they spoke to people in their dreams and gave warnings as when Joseph was told to leave to Egypt so that King Herod could not harm Jesus as a boy.

But that's how they have communicated with us human folks, but I never once considered how angels might speak with God. God is all knowing, as I have been taught and believe. Angels are God's assistants, guardians and informants, as I believe and have been taught again. I wondered if an angel had something on his mind, would he share it with God or leave it sit there for God to find since He knows everything anyhow?

My assumption now is the angels have their own way of

reaching out to God. Not just as a means of reporting back to God, but also to express their concerns and perhaps cite a rebellion just as in the case of Lucifer. With angels having a leg up on us in spiritual matters, I would also gather that they had a clearer way of sharing their mind with God.

When I was shown this picture method of praying from this unseen force, there was such a love in the air and great concern. I didn't see anyone or anything that pulled me to fixate on. Only a wonderful lesson and a great device to communicate better with God was shown.

When I first started to expand on the idea of this form of communication, I quickly realized that this manner of connecting was more than just a way of communicating with God. As I mentioned previously, the angels may even have meant that this is how they also communicated with each other.

Angels have been said to wander the Earth to help and guide people on various life tasks and issues. With angels having less than God's capacity to be everywhere and all knowing, I realized that they too had to give each other a holler every now and then. I highly doubt that they would whisk themselves to the other corner of the Earth just to tell the other angel they needed a hand with something. Cell phones are also not very likely to be a handheld commodity that they would invest in, either. Come to think of it, they would need a satellite or universal phone to traverse the ground they had to cover! God only knows what kind of bill they would have to pay for that sort of service.

Something had to be simpler and perfectly within their capabilities to express themselves to each other and to call for some assistance being that they are less than God in their strength. So it's logical to think that the angels must have their own unique and pure form of communication, and to me, it was a beautiful way to envision and pour one's emotion into a vision. To speak visually, wow, it just tells volumes in one scene.

To take a moment out of ones life and try to capture it by

writing it down, say in a book, does little when you are able to replicate it into a Michelangelo of a display. The saying goes that no one knows what you go through, except you and God. But wouldn't it be wonderful if we could speak as the angels do to show our experiences fully where there's no room for misinterpretation?

It would certainly hush any bundle of rumors or gossip if one were able to stick their head into the vibe of pictured thoughts and see for themselves what the truth was. It would be pure communication to attach ones emotions to our daily visuals and add it to the 'stream of thought' in our world. We would all truly know the hearts of man and who stood next to us. So much strife and harm could be avoided if we understood each other better and felt the cry for help when a person was in need or ready to lash out.

Just as in my lesson, I wasn't able to directly conceive of what was being asked in the prayers because they were not intended for me to hear them but I could sense their vibe. I believe there would be no invasion of privacy among people if there was a thought in the air not intended for everyone, but there would be an understanding to some level.

How lucky are the angels to have such a way to communicate and share with God and each other! Heck, and how lucky am I, that at least for the time being, I was able to practice and learn how to speak with God on a purer level of intent.

I know that my heart and mind is deeper and more complicated than anything I could put into words. There is so much that exists in me that has absolutely no words to define it, and yet there it sits and exists in me, still. There are many things that exist in this world just waiting to be discovered. Once they are discovered, we as humans like to place a label or title on it just so each of us knows what it is that we are speaking of if we so decide to speak on this new discovery. But I now knew that even if there were a bacteria of some sort, that had previously existed with no name, and yet it was ravaging my body making me gravely ill at the moment. I knew, had that happened to me, that God would only need me to point my heart to the problem with no name in mind and still know what I was meaning.

Meaning exists without words, and words can have so much less meaning than our heart. I had learned in life lessons, that the word "love" carried a lot of weight in the eyes of the world. It was always, "extend your love to the needy" and yet there were still needy people. Where was this love exactly if it was being asked for and spoken of all the time when I saw so much lacking in the area of love for so many bad things to exist?

The word "love" meant nothing without meaning and putting that meaning into action. Love is an emotion that can be felt and seen. It was not a word.

Now when I point my heart and thoughts to God, I feel I can truly send Him my love in a big squish of thoughts and images. After learning my lesson on praying in pictures, I didn't allow for words to even attempt to fully show what I meant when I shared my love for Him. I instead purely and simply shared a part of my life, which loved Him.

Much like a postcard with a stamp of emotions, my Picture Prayers were being sent to God from the convenience stores of my psyche on every corner. There was no "taking time to pray" because praying took no time at all!

In integrating Picture Prayers into my life, it initially took some thought to work my brain noodle into shape to envision what I sought in my prayers. It was a whole different thought process for me to think of what to envision, what was important and to hold all of these ideas in my head to do it right.

I think I made a bigger deal out of it than it was to be, obviously. It was kind of like sitting down to a new shiny computer keyboard. I knew where to place my hands and fingers, but I just couldn't stop looking down at my fingers to see them grace the new keys!

I knew the "ins and outs" of Picture Prayers, since it was ingrained in my mind from my wonderful experience. But I allowed myself to marvel just a bit too much in the beginning of my practicing praying in this manner. It was simply too fun, and there were way too many things I wanted to try it on to begin with which led me to snapping shots in my head of everything in life.

Narrowing down my focus was surely needed. So I began to try focusing on a couple of things from my present day, and then picking up a few things from the past to add into the mix of my Picture Prayers. I would think of things like how I needed the strength to focus on becoming a decent occupational therapist, how my car needed something to stop the rust from eating it up further, and then think of how I needed healing from a past pain in my life.

A quick focus on a visual that summed up my feelings about each topic then came into order. Like in the instance of my becoming a better therapist, I envisioned myself in my medical jacket examining a patient and suggesting the best approaches for them to get better. I then saw myself driving my rusty bucket of a car and how horridly embarrassing it was to drive that beast. Then I saw myself in sorrow, agonizing over an ordeal that left me feeling hung out in the cold.

I did just as I was shown in my Picture Prayer lesson, I gathered one snapshot at a time in my mind and thought of what I associated each picture to. I then thought of the next picture and then the next, and did the same to be sure I had encased my intentions to each mental photo. I then looked God's way and asked for the guidance I needed to continue making the right decisions in my life and to keep me strong. Then with my eyes wide open and my heart pounding hard, I focused my prayers to go forward to God and off I sent them. Of course, I remained dedicated in my taught tradition and out of respect for the One who helped us all;

I ended this and each prayer, "In Jesus' name. Amen."

In the beginning of my practicing Picture Prayers, they had already proven to me to be shorter and easier to arrange and send. As with anything, practice makes perfect. I felt my prayers becoming more and more full and fulfilling to me personally. I didn't feel that I had left out anything or anyone and felt satisfied in nodding off to sleep after my Picture Prayers at night.

Earlier in my life, I had tried to experiment in praying during the day since staying conscious to pray at night used to be such a challenge. Praying during the day at church was allowed, so I saw nothing wrong in trying to do a little bit of that myself. But as fate would have it, when you put your hands together or close your eyes during the daytime, people take notice. So it was a bit hard to be discreet about praying like that, so I started to get creative and prayed without the hand and eye thing. During those days my prayers became a lot more fulfilling for me since I could actually complete them and not feel disrespectful in my communication with God by falling asleep.

When Picture Prayers came into my life, I also started to use this form of prayer in the daytime. When I did that, I truly brought Picture Prayers to a whole new level. I felt more like I was having a conversation with God and lending my thoughts to what I was seeing as I was seeing it.

I could be walking down the street and stop by a coffee shop, as there were many near my side of town where I lived in Milwaukee, and see any number of things of prayer interest. I could see a less fortunate person out on the corner panhandling for change, and lend a thought to God about this person, right then and there. There was no having to wait until I went to bed at night and then having to reflect on the events of the day and what I was concerned with.

From major concerns to something that may seem minor to another person, I would take a look at it and give a glance to the heavens literally or in my mind and ask for a little help or understanding. From a tumbleweed of trash rolling down the street to a child throwing a tantrum in the middle of the grocery store with an embarrassed mom nearby, I lent a thought to God about the matter.

I soon found that I was not just praying at all times of day, but all day!

It has been nine years since I have learned to pray as the angels do, and it has done for me what I have never imagined. God is no stranger and speaking to God is no longer a strain or needing to take time for. Prayer is at all times, in each step and waking moment, I now feel like the top of my head is wide open to sending thoughts to God. To place a title to what has changed in me because of Picture Prayers or to even call it an act of doing something — is odd.

What is occurring now is just me being me, which is a creation of God who remains as that and doing what comes natural. Every thought, emotion, scene or act is all sent God's way. No line is drawn, there's no place where He's not allowed to see, because I know I am a flawed human being just as He knows. So to show shame in what I am and how I've been created to be isn't part of this for me. Showing that I can work for change and grow in the midst of my flaws and failures, helps make my shortcomings easier to open up to Him to have a look and help inspire me where I need it most.

Chapter 6

My Mind as a Guide

In making myself as an open door to God with my Picture Prayers in mind, I began to learn more about my life experience as a true observer and experiencer. Life became a surreal classroom and playground at the same time. I found structure and beauty in absolutely every crevasse!

A blade of grass didn't just sit in my hands without me pulling it up to the sunlight to have a closer look at the inner workings of its structure. Then I would think about things like how God couldn't even create a single piece of grass without decorating it with the most elaborate patterns to show off its life source. With my Picture Prayers, I began to get so comfortable with God that I would hold up something like that single piece of grass and ask if it was really necessary to create such intricate work in such a discreet area of life?!

Then I'd think about the even finer details in that blade of grass and wonder who even knew if man would gather the intelligence to create microscopes and machinery to see life up-close, even? I suppose God knew we would, but I don't know many people who pause to take in their surroundings, let alone some grass veins. But, I knew and appreciated that these creations and all creations weren't done in the manner they were to just please our human senses.

At some point I grew to slow down with such anal questions to God about why He created this or that to look this way over another. I instead admired His creations and complimented Him as being the greatest artist there ever was. For me, having been a comic strip, 3D, ceramic artist myself, there was no other way to explain why God put so much into what He created. He was of course doing what He did out of love, but He also appeared to find great joy in creating life full of color and harmony.

I just let my mind wander along in my communications with God! There was time now to do this with Him. I had already been able to address so many concerns with Him after exploring my personal Picture Prayers that were most pressing in my life. Now with prayer being so accessible, it didn't become a burden or strain anymore. Prayer became an asset, comforter and companion.

As a child, when I shared my bedroom with my sister, before going to bed each night we always remembered to tell each other, "Don't forget to pray." In a matter of six months of my praying in visuals, there was no reminding myself or taking time out for prayer. There was no regiment, although in the very beginning I would at times follow the habit of having my head bowed and eyes closed.

Prayer became second nature and an open forum. I only used my mind as a guide to bring me in front of curiosities I've always had in life but now I felt free enough to ask God about them. Being what I call an "info-maniac" I am constantly looking up odd facts and figures on various Internet search engines. But for the life of me, if I didn't write down something that I wanted to look up online, I sometimes would forget.

In daily life, I'm much the same in having a curiosity about this or that. I feel like I am always in that cute stage kids go through when they ask "why, why, why" about absolutely everything. When I'm not next to a computer to look up my topic of question, I now know to look to God for some guidance on the answer or for even a touch of enlightenment. I, of course, don't get a bellowing voice of instruction from Him, but it's nice to know He's there listening to my interest.

I hardly doubt anyone can keep up with my wandering mind and in-depth looking into blades of grass. So, yeah, at least there is a perceptive ear around to comprehend my fascinations with and about life.

Oddly enough, I truly got to know myself better on more levels than I knew to belong to me by practicing Picture Prayers. I am not a person who can sit and meditate to seek within or whatever it is that people say they can find in meditation. I have tried it, but I was only met with a good snooze and a shrugging of the shoulders on my behalf. I don't think I have a short attention span, but again, it's that old combination of getting comfy and closing of the eyes that spells out sleep to me.

With Picture Prayers, I didn't have to sit to get comfy or close my eyes to focus my attention. But I did have to look into my inner workings and see where I saw myself in life and what life was seeing in me. I had to lend some focus to gather some visuals and I often would get lost in what I was seeing.

Most especially if I took Picture Prayers into bed with me at night where I am laying down, I let my Picture Prayers go where they may. There have been several occasions where I have looked at an event that occurred in the day that bothered me and let the event play in my mind again. Sometimes there have been some really hairy instances that have bugged me and my Picture Prayers turned into movies to allow me to analyze the situation further.

For instance, while writing this book I moved to Melbourne, Victoria in Australia, the wonderful land down under (oh—do I miss it)! Due to a lovely delay of airplane flights from my hometown of Milwaukee, Wisconsin to Chicago, I was horrendously late to catch my next flight to Los Angeles. With ten minutes to spare after landing and Chicago O'Hare being the granddaddy of airports, I had to hightail it fast to catch my next flight!

In the midst of my crazy, sweaty, panting, panicked rush, I managed to get those folks to halt my next plane to throw my ravaged limbs aboard. Upon catching my breath and sliding my backside into my seat, I realized that I had lost at least one item in my run. It was my prized purple and yellow, squishy, bean bagged pillow that I had purchased just for the upcoming 14-hour flight to Melbourne from Los Angeles. I felt sick to my stomach when I realized that I was so preoccupied in making it to the flight that if I could drop something so large, what else could I have dropped along the way? With my things already tucked in the overhead compartment and little time between my landing, running off to the next flight and partially not wanting to add anymore to my stressful flight, I would not be able to answer that riddle until I arrived in Melbourne.

With Melbourne being 17 hours ahead of where I'd come from, and having the queen of all jetlags, I did all that I could do when I arrived in Melbourne. I dropped my luggage, crawled onto a bed and slept for 16 hours straight, the longest I'd ever slept in my life at one time! Yet I was still able to slip in and initiate a Picture Prayer over the concern of my having dropped something in my rushed state at the Chicago O'Hare Airport.

This Picture Prayer then turned into a movie where I fully saw myself running and dragging my laptop computer, my carry-on luggage and my coat wrapped around the handle of my luggage. I looked at my luggage; everything looked zipped up nice and tight as I quickly paced myself along. I then looked at my coat dangling, which had my missing pillow attached to it in the sleeve. All looked secure as far as the pockets of my coat were concerned, but I saw that my jacket had slipped to one side. It was able to shift too easily, apparently, and my pillow escaped onto free pavement and into the arms of some other lucky traveler, darn!

I hadn't lost anything else, according to what I could assess from my own thoughts and perhaps a good amount of calming from the Man above. I soon then found myself able to rest more at ease and securely and I got the best sleep of my life!

Upon waking, and having the strength to even get up, I looked through my things to assess if I had indeed lost anything else in my haste. Luckily, my Picture Prayer gave me the correct perspective. Knowing myself better through Picture Prayers was one thing, but to be able to have the calm to see situations from even another perspective was invigorating!

I was able to use my mind and God's guidance in a way that brought a new sense of peace and insight. It was like looking outside of myself for a moment, and then looking at everything from a more logical stance. I should say, it could appear to be more logical, but I am certain there's a spiritual aspect to it, as well. It just seems that right now my typed words are falling short of giving full meaning to what this aspect is exactly—so typical of words!

I'm finding that a lot these days: my mind can apparently only go to a certain extent before it shrugs its shoulders and attributes inspiring occurrences to God. Luckily, my mind doesn't pretend to be scientific and try to explain the formula to solving riddles that it has no business to lay claim to. I tend to become irritated with those scientific minds who believe they are so smart that nothing exists without it being labeled with a scientist's stamp of approval. If we knew all that there is to know, there would be no such thing as learning, and yet scientists still look to expand their knowledge so it seems they haven't learned it all. I suggest they take notes then, because God won't slow down just for them to keep up.

The spirit of God can't be measured in a cup and given limits to what He can and cannot do. If man can create on his own, and show that all can be explained through experiments, I would love to see that done without having any working tools already created here by God. Just to sit in a clean and sterile room, without any atom-sized elements or sunlight or clothing and have a go at creating something special. I doubt much would walk out of that room but a sorely beaten man with an overly large cranium, who hopefully became more humbled to what God can create.

The mind is only to be used as a guide. The heart and soul of us belongs to God. This is what I know, this is what I have learned, and this is now how I live. Worries happen, but again I know that is the mind at work dealing with the existence at hand. Thoughts of love for another and spiritual paths, this is my soul speaking and thinking, and these are my elements of most concern.

I know this life is like a classroom of sorts, where I get to use my mind to add to my journey of understanding. My mind can then help me translate experiences into love and connecting them to spiritual growth, or lack thereof. It is always up to me to decide on which way my life experiences will be allowed to affect the soul of me. Changing me for the better to get closer to under-standing my path to God or changing me to go away from God, this is what my mind is for.

Previously, I know I thought way too much about everything all of the time. Now I just let my heart wander and wonder, and let my mind and soul do their own duties. Harmony is not always consistent between the two parts of my mind and soul, but there is a working relationship always in progress. Had their job been complete, I would not be here anymore, so something still needs to be worked out.

I can't wait to see what more there is to learn, though pain, sorrow and loss is sure to come through, too. Love, birth, fun, and laughter will come, as well. Good can and will outweigh the bad, if my mind allows it to be remembered to have come and have it be taken for what it is, which is relief given from God.

Chapter 7

God's Answers

I have always been taught to ask God for help in practically any circumstance. "Ask, and you shall receive," is a saying told to me always by any number of people. Then there's the saying, "God helps those who help themselves!" Now I don't know where that saying came from, but it seems to be saying that we need to get off our backsides to help in the process of God helping us.

But which is it? I ask God and I get the help I need or I have to work for the help I need? I didn't know whether to be faithful and just pray my mouth dry, or to work until there was no sweat left in my pores!

Here's a saying I wish I could have thought up as a little girl when I was hearing all of these lovely phrases, "Don't confuse a child!" I don't know if any of these sayings are Biblically able to be applied to every situation in life, but as a kid I still felt it was a cruel joke to say such phrases as a cover to all inquiries. In either case, it didn't help me to understand much more then.

Knowing a little better now, I know God helps those who don't always ask and those who don't always help themselves. I didn't know to ask God to teach me how to pray visually, and I surely didn't know how to help myself in praying better than I was. God didn't mind, and He still saw to it that I got the message by way of His messengers.

When I went to church while growing up, it varied which denomination church I attended depending on whether my parents felt up to dropping us kids off or having us walk to the nearest church. Yet, it didn't matter what church I went to, I got a similar message at almost every sermon. The pastor of the church would generally announce, "God told me blah, blah, blah!"

Now, I was amazed that God had so much to say to so many people for one, but also that each pastor was so darn fortunate to meet God! I would always wish that these pastors would go into more detail about these Godly encounters, like what God was wearing, did He really have a throne He sat on, does He eat meat; just logical questions, of course. But no, they would just speak about what they were told by God to say to the congregation of the church. It was a bit disappointing to not get more info, but I gathered that they just didn't have time to explain it all in the middle of the sermon. However, I did get to see how one pastor reacted to what he thought was a Godly encounter, at least.

One evening, my high school aged Sunday school class had the run of the church while we practiced for our Christmas play. We were going over our lines diligently under the watchful eye of our teacher, when we decided to goof off a bit. One of the guys in my class I'll call "Jerry" was going through his changes and getting a nice bellowing voice as he entered into manhood. The class got a kick out of him transitioning from a squeak to this baritone and would often get him to blast out something with his new windpipes.

Our teacher had stepped out of the room for a moment while we all stood in the pulpit of the church. We got the grand idea to turn the microphone on to let Jerry have a go at hearing his voice over the speakers. So Jerry belted out some made up sermon starting off with something like, "I have come to you to give you a message..." We chuckled quietly as Jerry carried on slow and methodically to emphasize each bellowing word.

Then, out of nowhere, tearing up the basement stairs to our shock comes our church's pastor. He was all wide-eyed and bewildered as he entered and walked slowly up one of the aisles toward us. Then he looked up to the front of the church and saw Jerry and the rest of us frozen like a deer caught in headlights.

The pastor suddenly broke into laughter and sputtered in-between the laughs that he thought the Lord started speaking to him so he came running to see what He wanted. We all then started to laugh so hard I thought that I would crack a rib!

This incident made me wonder even more if when these pastors said that the Lord (or God) spoke to them, that they meant the Lord really spoke out loud like Jerry did and if He sounded anything like Jerry? Besides, when these pastors said the word "Lord" did they mean Jesus or God, anyhow? It seemed to be interchangeable, and that didn't make any sense to me since God was the Father and Jesus was His Son. Two differently named entities with two different roles in the Bible, and then there was a Holy Spirit that got into the mix, too, and to call them all a Trinity? When I looked at this all from a kid's perspective again, why learn all three names if they were all the same? Oh the headaches I created for myself as a child, let me tell you!

But anyhow, I was always wondering what it was like for the "Lord" to speak to a person. I wanted elaboration, a picture painted, a story told, just something to say what these pastors meant by this claim. Why wouldn't God speak to me so directly as He did for the pastors, was there something wrong with me?

Later on in my teenage years, I understood more of what was meant by the claim of God speaking to a person. I hadn't directly noticed it so much before, that is, until I really needed an answer. In fact, my very soul depended on an immediate answer at least one time in my existence.

I have what I call "waking dreams" which are so-called dreams that seem so real, that it's sometimes hard to accept that they did not actually happen. These waking dreams are so revealing and moving that the content of them feel like they are adding to my life experiences. Waking dreams can be tests, lessons, or even adventures that all seem to relate to the survival of my body, soul or others.

One waking dream consisted of what I consider to be the ultimate test on my faith. I remember suddenly finding myself in an extremely large mansion of a house that was rather empty except for the presence of my younger sister. The mansion was mostly painted in white, with pale wooden floors throughout. There was even an ever present light from each crevasse of all the rooms that I could see, as if no ceiling or roof existed where direct sunlight could beam through.

I remember watching my sister walk into the next room from where I stood, when suddenly the door to the room I was in slammed shut! I backed up carefully onto a bed in the center of this large empty room, as I felt darkness completely surround and envelope me like a supernatural cloud. The darkness became so thick that I could barely even see the surface of the bed I was now kneeling upon as if to brace myself for whatever might come next. Then suddenly and violently with no gentle initiation, the bed began to rise and slam back down to the floor!

I felt so cutoff from everything; my sister, the light and even' my freedom to leave that room.

Without thinking twice, my mind and my heart immediately turned to God as I began to pray silently in my heart for His protection to save me from whatever darkness had taken me hostage. I felt as if God's eye quickly glanced my way, and in a rush upon seeing what was happening, He gave me my freedom back! Merely seconds into my throwing my heart up in prayer, the bed became calm and settled back onto the floor and the door to the room swung open where pure light shone in and conquered the darkness as it created what looked like a golden path of light back into the mansion.

I crept slowly off the bed, and placed my feet onto the path of light and walked into the hallway. As soon as I stepped from the room, I looked to my left to see my sister sitting comfortably on the floor of another large room as if she were watching something spectacular in front of her on a television set. When she saw me, she turned my way and smiled as if she were proud I pulled through the test okay.

To be honest, I was a bit perplexed why she made no attempt to help me since there was no way she didn't hear what I'd just gone through. Exhausted, I walked slowly her way and sat down by her side on the floor, curling my legs to one side and sighing to catch my breath. The ordeal was as real as anything else in my life, and I felt then in that waking dream, as I do now, that I was fighting for my very soul.

Had I not thought to go into prayer to seek God, I don't think I would have come out of that challenge alive. It felt as if a choice was made; for me to allow the darkness to have me and feel its strangle-hold on me, or to reach to higher grounds and have faith that God would indeed help me when I needed Him most. There was a confidence, such a leaning on God from my end to show me the way back home, and He did with no hesitation. That's the God I got to know following this incident, among others, that God is one to show He is with us when we show we are with Him!

Although this story is hard for me to even think of having happened, I will always marvel at God's speedy response. I know what my predicament was and how close I felt to there being no return in my situation, and God was there with me the whole while.

Perhaps the saying was correct, "Ask and you shall receive." It took only seconds before God answered my prayer, but He had already put things into motion before I had asked, too. Perhaps the whole experience was done just to use as the example for this chapter, to strike the right chord in others to see the miracle of prayer since He knew I'd be writing this book before I did.

It truly was no less than a miracle what took place for me, but God's answering me isn't always so direct and knowing. Yet, when I have listened to my pastors, it sure sounded like direct chatting going on to me. Again, though, I now realize that God can move you to the right answers.

That saying, "God helps those who help themselves," also now makes more sense to me. It's not about fully reaching with my own hands to find spiritual answers. But if I reach for an answer like God helping me in my situation in some form, there is a more than likely chance of something being moved in my direction to find it like that path of light He showed through the darkness in my waking dream.

It's like my daily task of not placing my glasses where I can find them. It's an odd scenario and pretty ironic that here I am having a hard time seeing and needing to go searching for the object that would help me see better! Sometimes the searching seems futile, but if I don't make the effort to find my glasses, there's a guarantee that I won't see clearly. By reaching for and finding my tool of sight, I see. By not making an effort in reaching my glasses, I don't see. By being more organized and putting my glasses in the same spot so I don't have to search to begin with, now this is a learning process!

Seeking out God does take some effort, but I have learned that He will meet me half way if I let Him. In learning how to pray visually, I have also taken notice of how God has spoken to me all along. Praying in pictures was new to me, but apparently, it was nothing new to Him.

Chapter 8

God's Visual Insight

Yes, seeing and packaging prayers up to be sent to God was new to me. Being that I was taught this method from an angelic presence, it should have been obvious to me that God was not new to this method of communication. Of course, I understood that He was able to comprehend the picturesque prayers sent His way, but I never thought about Him sending them back at me!

There seems to be a consensus that people who believe in God, believe that He speaks with and to us. Just as my pastors from church spoke of God sending messages to them with some regularity going on. Without having heard a lot of details about how exactly God had answered or spoken to people who surrounded me on a day-to-day basis, I have had to assume certain aspects on this phenomenon prior to my better understanding of how God worked.

It seemed to me that there was a private understanding between people and God, and the interpretations of what was really an answer from God. I supposed an answer could be anything from what a person deemed as a sign from God, or a sudden occurrence that remedied a situation at hand. Then there are the direct miracles where healing has taken place where even the scientists might have to admit defeat in being able to determine how a medical healing had occurred.

It appeared, and according to myself and others, that God had His ways of speaking volumes when He wanted and when it was appropriate.

When I began to discover more about myself while I built myself up to be a more visual person for Picture Prayers, true recollections of communication from God came to me. No, I didn't see any billowing clouds or throne of gold, but I surely had seen and experienced something wonderful. In fact, I had seen a lot of things in life that prompted and inspired me that I know had Godly connections.

I now remembered countless moments where I was undecided on what to do, where to turn, or if I should give up on many occasions during what seemed like dire situations. I think at some point in everyone's life comes a "mystery inspiration", or direct visualization that gets a person to believe they will get through the problem presented to them at the time. There have been many mysteries of inspiration in my life, and there's one that stands out from the rest because it came at a time when my career path was at stake.

I was uncertain what I should major in while attending college at the University of Wisconsin-Milwaukee; it was truly a hectic time in my life. I had started out as an art student, being that my goal in life was to draw cartoons and comic strips to exhibit my passion for silliness for all to see. After attending art classes for a little over a year, I decided that drawing the required apples and trees just wasn't getting me to any level of silly drawings fast enough. So I figured I would keep up with my drawings in my own time, and I actually did get to draw comic strips for more than a dozen newspapers at one point.

The challenge was then to actually find a course of study that didn't involve much math (I was terrible at it); yet something challenging (Since I was supposedly an advanced student in high school). I had tried a few courses here and there to see what other degrees would be like to attain, only to find them to be too easy, boring, or limiting as a career. I wasn't a scholar, but when you can avoid even buying the books for class and pass with good grades, something was wrong.

A friend of a friend then told me that she was studying to be an occupational therapist. She explained to me how it helped people physically, emotionally, and it involved creativity and science, all the things I could really enjoy doing and handle. She really needed to say no more! It was only the beginning of the semester so I was able to still add a class that was required to be an occupational therapy student.

The first day of my attending this particular class, I sat down, pointed my eyes to the instructor and waited to see what this was all about. Only a few minutes into the talk, something highly out of the norm (even for me) passed before my eyes. I got a distinct visual in my head or right in front of me, where I saw myself walking across an old fashioned, wood stage, accepting my Bachelor of Science degree in occupational therapy! I don't mean that I imagined that I would someday get my degree. I mean I *saw* myself accepting my degree in full graduate robes and all!

The vision came and went quickly as I remained in my seat slightly gasping and looking around discreetly as if to see if anyone else saw what I did. After anxiously sitting through the class and hardly being able to focus on what was taught since my mind flooded with thoughts about what this vision meant. When I saw myself graduating as a therapist, there was such a confidence that this is what God intended for me to be.

I was so moved by the vision I had seen that immediately following the class, I had all of my classes changed to attain my degree in occupational therapy. I knew that I had received this guidance from God, and I didn't question it. However, there were a lot of issues that came up much later where I could have doubted what I had witnessed in class that day as being my future. Like the grand-daddy issue of me failing my first major science course of Anatomy and Physiology. Not only had I failed it that first time, but I took it again and failed it yet again! I had never had to truly study for anything, so I had no idea what I was up against in having to learn every anal detail about the human body. When I took the same class a third time, I learned how to study for the first time in my life and have nailed A's (or near A's) ever since!

Unfortunately, I had not taken school totally seriously up until that point, and my grade point average reflected it. In order to get into my area of study at the University of Wisconsin-Milwaukee, they took only the top students with the best grades. That translated into being 3.725, which was the lowest point average that was usually accepted into the program. All other folks applying who were rejected would have to wait their turn on a never-ending waiting list, retake some courses to raise their A-'s into straight A's or give up fully by changing their course of study.

Well, I knew what I was shown by God and what He had intended and how it felt to me; I would graduate as an occupational therapist and nothing less! The only thing I didn't know was how I was to get into the program, and what wooden stage I would be walking across since my present university didn't use one like that for graduation. When I saw there was no definite way I would get into my school's program, I contacted another college and asked them what I needed to get accepted. This other school then took a close look at all of my transcripts and told me that I would have to take a full year of their courses of 36 credits and get nothing less than an A- for each specified class. Then, *if* I qualified, I would have to go through an interview and application process.

I thought about what this school reported to me, and then I had another look at what I recalled of the picture God had given me on the path I was to be on. There was absolutely no room for error if I was to go on faith alone to this school. I had never nailed straight A's before; heck-I hardly knew what that would look like!

By some miracle and a lot of faith stuffed behind it, I pulled it off!

I attended Mount Mary College, an all women's Catholic college where theology courses fashioned by the School Sisters of Notre Dame, came as a side dish and main course to my education. I took my required courses, adjusted my shock when instructors knew my name in these smaller classes, nailed my A's, and literally danced my way across an old fashioned, wood stage (exactly as I had seen it in my vision) and became an alumni!

To say my success in school was all based on a vision given to me—well—it really isn't a stretch to assume that. But it was more than that, there was a deep knowing in me that sensed it was a pure message, with God written all over it. Faith built up in me that this was meant to be in my future, I didn't know how and I had to work to find that path, but I did. I was given a hint, a slight peek into the possibilities and it was as right-on as it was meant to be.

By the way, God guided me to a great career as an occupational therapist, too! Not only do I get to help people get physically, emotionally and mentally better after an illness or injury, but I also have great freedom. My career has allowed flexibility unlike many do, where I am able to travel across the country (even internationally) if I choose, or take time off between contracted work to pursue my writings or give lectures. It has truly been the most suitable and enjoyable career to accommodate my other passion to write and help others on more spiritual matters.

Since my career guidance, I have since had several pictures sent to me that have guided me to look further in one direction over another. I used to believe some of these instances were somehow intuition or even little psychic episodes. Perhaps some of them are coming from somewhere deep inside of me and with all of my attributes being created by God, it's still Him. I don't own anything in this life, and anything given to me is a gift.

I have said so many times to anyone who will listen, that God isn't done speaking to us yet. The Bible has been written where the Word lives on but God's actions continue to grow through us each day. There's still so much to learn in life and so much more that God can show us. I believe it's essential for me to remain open to Him and any new words or guidance He would like to teach.

God is not just the God of Moses, Noah, or Abraham; He is my God, too. In being my God, He is alive and active in my life today, creating new lessons and gaining full respect, love and laughter from me more and more with each passing minute. The insight He chooses to send with special emphasis is always breathtaking for me, and an absolute honor to witness. I am on my tiptoes in hopes that I can give some smidgens of inspiration for other people without talking over anyone's head, just by letting others see and hear what God has let come my way.

Chapter 9

Practice in Pictures

As long as I can remember, I have had a fascination with drawing. I remember my first masterpiece in drawing, because it amazed my kindergarten teacher so much that I was able to draw my favorite animal so well, a bunny. I don't know what it was about with rabbits and me, but I loved them, and Bugs Bunny has and always will be my favorite cartoon character. I mean Bugs Bunny just has character that has stretched him into everything from pantyhose to a boxing ring, with few to follow his flexibility.

In having an appreciation for the art of writing and the art of art itself, I know that I tend to take interest in things that many others don't. People who are visual artists, look at the art in life so that they can interpret what they see to duplicate or create it on a canvass of sorts. Then comes along the non-artists who simply marvel at the ability of artists who can actually create art and see such detail in life where they can literally create something recognizable enough where others can identify what it is.

Me being an artist (still to some degree), I've always looked at the marveling non-artists and thought how odd it was that they found drawing recognizable objects to be such a tremendous talent. Of course artists have talent to create art, but not to see art.

The questions would always come my way about how I was able to capture a mood or an angle so perfectly in my drawings, but again, it was all about seeing it first and then being able to create something from it. I wasn't creative enough to know what a grumpy person would look like; I first saw it across someone's face and was able to interpret it myself into a cartoon image. I didn't have to always look at a grumpy person to draw the cartoon either; I knew what it looked like already from my life experience. All I did was pay attention to what I saw in life, and kept it in mind.

Artists often get labeled as being visual people, and that is true. But artists are also people who take the time to see details and remember them, or look at them directly to duplicate. There is no trick to the trade of being an artist, unless it is to be able to pay attention to detail. Then there's that little connection between mind and body to be able to tell one's hand what to draw, but that's a whole other book.

I thought about how it would be to explain to a group of people how to do Picture Prayers on their own. Then I thought about how I had done a few lectures to kids and parents on how to draw cartoons. After the talks, a few parents expressed how they enjoyed the demonstration but that they would leave it up to the people who are more visual than they were to actually do drawings.

Visual?

If I'm not mistaken, that means having eyeballs and the ability to interpret what it is you are seeing. But I knew what they meant, yet, even a person who draws a straight line or circle is an artist. A stick figure is a work of art; it was conceptualized and created where no one had done such a thing on the same spot ever before. By choice of taste makes the drawing a masterpiece or not, and if the artist loved it, I say give it a blue ribbon!

I know that some people might be deemed as being better at

envisioning a scene in their heads than the next person. I bet I could sit in front of a room full of people and say, "Try imagining a beach with the Sun setting over it." There would be that one person who says they just are not the type to be able to see anything in their head, but I bet they could imagine something! I don't care if they could imagine a hole in their shirt or a cement block, something could be seen in their head if they really just sat and tried.

People have the ability to see with their eyes closed!

As I understand it, God doesn't give us abilities just for the heck of it. There had to be a reason why He chose us to be able to find a nice patch of green grass, lay down to stretch out to look up at the beautiful sky, close our eyes and *still* see the beauty as if our eyes were still opened.

What the heck is that about?

Hey, I shared that I like to let my mind wander off into questioning why things are, and my mind just went there again.

There is always a reason for everything, and sometimes we are able to find out those reasons. Often times, there are many possibilities as to why things exist as they do, but we as people like to lay claim that there is only one reason for any single aspect of mystery in this life. So then this is my claim; perhaps we were always meant to use this ability in our daily lives and prayer might be one of its uses. But my head isn't big enough to say that praying in pictures is the only reason why we have the ability to see other things with our eyes shut or while looking at something else.

Now there's another interesting fact, I know that I can simply be looking at something to eat in my refrigerator and see in my head something else I would like to eat that is not in my fridge! I hardly doubt anyone can argue with me on that fact, because I don't know one bold faced person who hasn't had a craving for something not in their home at the moment. Some get so inspired by their mental and physical craving that they are turning their wanted food-image into action and are jumping in their car to head toward the nearest craving provider.

It almost sounds like a turning of visuals into action, to me. Actually, it sounds very much like what I do a lot of the time when I don't see what I want at home, I go out and get it.

I might be an artist with a supposed heightened sense for visuals, but I'm not the only one. If commercials on television didn't work with all of those scrumptious dishes of food they exhibit to add to people's cravings, there would be no such thing as food commercials. Truth be known, I have been living in a world where visual stimuli has been prompting me into action all of my life. That can only mean then, if I were to stand in front of a group of folks to tell them about Picture Prayers and how to do it, they already have a means to do it. We've been practicing it all of our lives, in one form or another, whether anyone will admit to it or not.

So, I'm just going to think out loud here for a bit and talk this out on how I might present the topic of Picture Prayers to others. With food being a great motivator, if I were sitting at a roundtable discussion, asking people to close their eyes and imagine a triple scoop of their favorite ice cream, I think it would only take moments for that visual to pop-up. Then to think of the texture, the feeling of that first bite of ice cream sliding down their throat and hitting bottom!

Geesch, I'm getting hungry just writing it down! Snack break for me, I'll be right back (and I'm not kidding—I'm pushing away from my desk now)!

Okay, I'm back now.

In rereading what I wrote, I can see how the emotions of such a relatable visual can get things stirred up (like belly yearnings). The picture of ice cream or whatever favorite food would be easy to conjure up, and automatically the thought of liking what is seen comes with it. So there you have it, a picture with emotions attached, but not exactly a Picture Prayer. I don't know if God would get a kick out of knowing what favorite snacks there are to have on this earthly plane, but it is a start.

If just a little practice is put into imagining things that are easy, and allowing the emotions associated to them to come forward, I think I might actually be able to get this across the right way to people. I have friends who are giggle queens and cannot hold a straight face for nothing when it comes to anything serious, myself included. So I know taking a step for focus might have to come in there for people who are a little off the beaten path of being able to hold a smile back.

Hmm, so what would I do in that case since I'm thinking aloud still anyhow? Well, I'm looking at my laptop computer screen right now. If I were to close my eyes like this, I can still imagine what my computer looks like. Maybe a little practice with eyes opened and then eyes closed, might be in order to get use to seeing detail in what is in our life. Then, a little thought could be considered about what is felt about the object that is being looked at. Like my laptop here, it's blue. I've been sitting here since before the Sun went down and now the Sun is down and I have no lights on so the room is dark. So what do I think of my computer now? Well, it's giving me the only light in the room, which is a good thing. The screen is crisp and clear against the darkness around me, but I can hardly see the blue frame of the computer anymore. But it's a cute computer, so that's what I think of it; it's cute.

So my eyes are open, then I close them. I can see the computer still in my mind and I think it's cute. Now it's all in one bundle of thought now, and I have my little package. Hmm, that worked well for me, now I just have to get it out of my head so I can focus to write more here. "Cute computer," thoughts are taking over my psyche now—great!

Okay then, so now I have a method to share that seems to

work even on me. Whenever I think on how I might explain anything to people where there is a ton of room to find no reason for it, I like to play with words. For me, it's fun to see the angles of thought that people may have in approaching something new.

For example if someone asked me, "Why imagine or envision anything when you can just spit out what you mean out loud? I would then ask, "Why do we have paintings on the walls in our homes instead of just long descriptions of what a painting would look like hanging there?"

I know that as a race of species, we find joy in visuals, and they are a lot less boring than words. I know that when I prayed before learning Picture Prayers, I would often envision what it was I was praying about, but I still let my words interpret everything. I also know that Jesus even used words to express Himself, but if even I envisioned in my prayers what I meant sometimes, wouldn't He? He was like us humans in some ways, so perhaps we both have similar capabilities given by our Father.

I think for anyone who has prayed there has always been more than just words coming forward. I know that tears of emotion, thoughts of love, and gut wrenching agony have been brought into prayer by myself and others. Luckily, God is all knowing and has heard, felt and seen everything we intended. I just feel better knowing that I am encompassing all of these same elements into my prayers with all of the senses He gave me to practice with.

Chapter 10

Photo Prayers

When I was a kid, it changed who I was to be told about praying. As young as I was, it inspired change in me to be a better human being to know that I was speaking to God (even with my resentment regarding my mom). To be completely honest, it also helped that my dad told me my guardian angel would rat me out if I did something bad, too. I'm not kidding either, that threat kept me from at least crossing the street without an adult around. My dad had a big thing about that going on when I was growing up for some reason, something about the risk of me being hit by a car; go figure ☺.

It was important to me, though, about the praying end bit and that I knew about it. I often wondered if other kids knew that they could pray to God for all kinds of situations, too. I especially thought of it when I would see kids bullying others and cause tears to stream down another kid's face. I felt bad for the ones who got pushed around, or picked on for being heavy, looking different or even being the quiet sort.

As an adult I still tend to wonder if other people resort to God for even the small things and problems in life. While in college, I really branched out to find that there were a lot of different religions out there and even how some members created groups on campus for their particular beliefs. I thought this was all highly interesting, but then dismaying when those different groups often tended to only hang out with their members. This was a phenomenon not only done by different religious groups, but even more noticeably by different ethnic groups organized on campus, as well. Being a multiracial person myself, I didn't always understand the necessity of this separation. Besides, I'd have to be cut up into different little morsels in order to be categorized properly.

Here I had come to college, all wide-eyed and looking forward to meeting different types of people, only to feel like I wasn't similar enough and therefore unwelcome by these various defining groups. It wasn't like there was a huge sign on these groups saying not to approach them, but they didn't feel all that approachable just because I could clearly see the click they were in. I shouldn't categorize all of the groups this way, of course. Then there were members of the college religious cults that were quite open and welcoming, but pushy, just the same.

One of the stranger aspects of some of the people I met in college, were the kids who were raised with no religious background. I don't mean they didn't claim any denomination or choose to not identify with a religion. I am meaning that no one, not a soul ever told them or encouraged anything about having a belief in anything, nada—zilch!

It was like meeting a blank piece of soul paper walking around, where no scribbles or even squabbles of faith could be seen! They had no sense of what to believe, no argument to dispute about faith, just a, "Yeah, so what" kind of attitude. I had never seen anything like it before, and it blew my mind!

It was hard to believe that no one took the time to teach them about their inner workings; what made them function from the inside out. I don't mean their insides as in guts and anatomy either, since even the physicians call their medical practices a "practice". Which could only mean that doctors don't have it down to "perfection" just yet, if and when they do I hope to get a call from someone to let me know. But "practicing" some sort of faith or religion I thought that was universal, although imperfect. Anyhow, I remember thinking that these religion lacking kids really must have had crappy parents, or been surrounded by people who didn't find it a big deal themselves.

In thinking about Picture Prayers and the possibility of my ever having children of my own, I know that I would want to teach them what I have learned about faith. I don't know if I would fully subject them to sitting in an hour-long sermon every Sunday, but I didn't see anything wrong with them learning on their level in Sunday school. Then in thinking about how I was taught about Picture Prayers, I knew that it would present a unique challenge in teaching my kids the principles of how to pray in this manner.

Kids in general are very imaginative in nature, I know, but anything taking longer to learn than it does to turn on a light switch in relation to prayer, just might not fly! But I know that I would need a way to at least show my kids how to keep in touch with God and share their lives with Him openly. So I thought and prayed on this matter, since getting ahead of myself even before having any children, is just my nature.

I don't know how long I pondered this question before I did the smack against the forehead bit in realization. The answer was sitting in front of me the whole time and of course my mind was off wandering about something else before I let it hit me. Praying in pictures, is praying in pictures!

If taken in the literal sense, a picture is a drawing, a painting or even a photograph! Children love to look at pictures or photos; it can keep their attention not just in one sitting but even in repeated sittings. Just as the children who have their favorite children's book with the same drawings and story over and over, photos are engaging for them.

If I had a child, I know I would be able to show them a photo of say Aunt Wanda and tell them, "Now ask God to keep Auntie Wanda healthy and her cat friendly." Then the next photo can be a picture of our family and I could suggest, "Tell God we are a happy family and we would like to keep it that way." Okay, so my actual suggestions would be a little less suggestive which I'm sure I'll get more practice in once a child comes into my life.

"A Picture Prayer Book," how perfect and essential that would be to have in my home! Just to get a little photo album and to select the pictures together for the prayer for the evening, would help organize and complete the prayers for my child.

If my child will be anything like me, she will certainly learn to love God and have a more than active conscience. I personally wouldn't want guilt to ever interfere into her life or mind when it came to the relationship she had with God. I think I would have eaten it up to have a way to guide my thoughts while in prayer as a child.

Not only would it have been a more fun adventure, full of color, life and direction to follow along with my thoughts for each of the photos I fingered through for my prayers. But it would have been something I would look forward to in anticipation that I could look through some photos with my parents to put in My Picture Prayer Book for God for the night. Any amount of time spent as a family unit, looking to God, I don't see as wasted time.

I hope to inspire others to know and see that there are other options out there to help make communicating with God, make sense for children. Scaring me into praying and speaking the same prayers said millions of times over by others didn't really hit home with me as a child. Only when I took some initiative to explore other options with my sisters, did it become more personal and truly meant something to me.

I don't know if saying that I had more control over my spiritual path is exactly the right way of expressing how it made me feel to even consider trying to speak differently in my prayers while growing up. I think the best way is to say that I felt that I had more freedom, and in knowing and feeling it was a choice, more dedication to God came out of me than I knew was even there! I even surprised myself, at times.

"Dedication" is a good word for what came out of me when I owned up and aimed to make my connection to God unique. Just as unique as each person's genetic makeup is, I feel that each person's connection to God is meant to be varied. There is no cookie cutter type of personality maker in God's universe, where another person can be said to view the world and react to it in the exact same way. Not even identical twins have the same views, and God made us that way for a reason.

No two thought patterns, no two finger prints, no two ears, no two nothings that spell individual people with individual lives are the same (yes twins have the same DNA but that's another story). Was this a mistake that we were made to be different to absolutely everyone? I highly doubt God would continually make the same mistake over and over again if we were meant to do as the next person does for any topic in life. God knew we wouldn't do that, but He was sure to show the way to Him and that it was attainable. Yet, if there was only one path to take to reach God, I would suspect that there would then be only one character in the Bible. Instead, there were various people written about with all sorts of backgrounds and odd stories to tell on how they came about and turned to God.

Thieves, a murderer of Jesus' followers (Saul later known as Paul), Roman soldiers, tax collectors, Rabbi's, rulers, commoners, gentiles; all sorts of people took a different path to finding the path with God. How I got started on my path may be different or not even considered strict enough to be perceived as acceptable by others to reach God. How I propose to teach my future children might also not be seen as the best policy in creating a smooth road for them to God. All I know is that we all have to start somewhere, somehow, in some manner to seek God out. At least I know that much is good enough for God.

Chapter 11

The Dance of Prayers

If there was a dance that my prayers could do, it wouldn't involve anything having to do with the forbidden dance of the Lambada, and the Macarena is too rehearsed. I think my prayers would look more like a mix between the graces of ballroom dancing, only to throw in a heap of breakdancing in the middle! Some things could be predictable, while other parts of the prayer could have a mean freestyle.

In ballroom dancing, there is a certain style that lets you know what form of movement you are going to be involving yourself in. Just as in praying in general, it is what it is so you know what you are aiming to do. Then there's breakdancing where you don't know exactly what's going to happen, but whatever it is, it's going to be good. For me, the blending in of Picture Prayers involves no routine, but it's all aimed for good!

Over the years, as I changed and grew in my prayers I learned that praying isn't to be used as a display. It's not something to grand stand just to show that it's being done, or even to be spoken about to others as if to demonstrate that one person is more dedicated to God than the other person. I'm not directing this at prayer led in church where the passion of a prayer is directed and increases strength in numbers; I see that as a positive. But when it comes to the person that uses their practice of prayer as a sort of demeaning weapon, that's where I have a problem.

I have had heart-to-heart discussions with people about issues in my life where I truly was looking for some good old fashioned advice, of the earthly sort, even. But out of some luck of the draw, I've had a few people that I've spoken to about life issues suggest that for me to have the problem I did that I must not have been praying enough! There were times even where the person instructed me on what Bible quotes to recite or read on to get my matter resolved and get me right with God.

Sometimes, if I was talking to someone I knew in person, they would hurriedly finger through a nearby Bible and read from it or ask me to. With the Internet being handy, I've even been in Christian chat rooms where suddenly my screen is filled with loads of Bible quotes to help see me through my ordeal. In either case, I truly understand the passion that others have where they intend to be truly helpful in their efforts. But out of what magician's hat did they pull out their conclusion that I wasn't praying enough or in the right way?

I don't think I could ever sit high enough to look down at somebody and judge with certainty that their prayers just weren't making the cut. We all have our opinions and can even apply our own suggestions for others to pray this prayer or that way; but to make a judgment call is a bit much. At times, I have been so caught off guard with prayer discussions brought into the conversation at hand, that it really turned me off with some people.

Had I asked someone, "Excuse me, what do you suggest I pray about to make my life better?" Then I could understand suggestions being brought my way for prayer, but it is still less likely that I would ask such a thing. I, as well as others, have been blessed with God's guidance to pray what I feel. The Bible has also been a wonderful guide for me to find help and the understanding I need about life's issues.

I'm a firm believer that people with good intentions to bring people closer to God in prayer, should be subtle in their approaches. If I'm talking about an issue with someone who believes prayer is the answer to everything, then a mere reminder can be made like, "Did you pray about it?" Not this whole ordeal of whipping out a Bible like, "Well you should look at this and let me cram this chapter down your throat although you didn't ask for it with your mouth agape in shock right about now—but still I'm going to just carry-on like I don't see that happening."

The oddest thing of all is; I truly understand this kind of passion. I feel like I have a million torches of fire filled passion for God, Jesus and prayer, burning in the center of my chest at any given time of the day! Heck, I wish I could scream from the International Space Station for all to hear what I have learned about prayer, where I would have no regrets in doing so. Yet, in being a conscience human being, I like to look at what I do from another's perspective. If I were me looking at myself floating outside the Space Station with a xylophone in hand screaming about prayer, I would think this woman must have been exposed to some alien bacteria or something!

Back to being me and someone who really wants to relate anything God connected, I know that there is a time and place for everything. If someone asked me to be a guest speaker at the Space Station to talk about Picture Prayers, then it was more welcomed that way. Not everyone would want to hear what I had to say, even those at the Station, but at least the people there wouldn't wonder what made me bring that subject up out of the blue since they actually asked for me to. There'd be no surprises or awkward moments of me introducing my way of looking at life issues and prayer, such as I've had to bear witness to in seeking advice.

Truly though, in my wanting to share my new approach to prayer, whenever those times of opportunity may arrive, I know that some amount of invite has to be there from others.

Cramming or shoving faith doesn't seem to work as well on the inside, more routines and habits seem to get formed on the outside from such acts—although further searching may also be inspired from some pushing such as in my case. However, it's more of our "insides" that has to want the information and inspiration being offered up, and this is something I really know now.

I could speak about people needing to pray more in any fashion they'd like, until I grew chest hair and neither would happen if there weren't certain markers in place. One marker being a willingness in spirit, while the other simply being a DNA marker in order to occur to a noticeable stage. Altering ones spirit isn't something I feel any single person is able to do to another from the outside if they are not allowed inside.

If this were possible, then all drug addicts had to do was go through a rehabilitation program without putting much thought into it. This indeed does happen quite a bit, and the addict usually goes back to their old habits later. It's not until the addict doesn't want to be an addict anymore that they succeed in rehabilitation. Years of friends and family pleading with a drug addict, just doesn't reach them until they reach themselves.

With all of the good intentions people have in their faith to make things better in other people's faith, may not succeed if it's not sought by their target of intention. It's something that I've had to accept with a lot of things I've learned and seen in this life. It's not easy either, to sit by and wish you could just change the way people live or think. It physically hurts me to see people not reaching out to God or even knowing He's there.

There's such a fine line of where it's safe to cross to speak to people about God and prayer, where even I have felt offended by people's approaches to me when they thought I needed their faith impressed upon me. No one knows the soul or prayer practices of an individual, and to assume that I or anyone else knows for certain can blow any chance of helping out. I feel the best thing I can do is to come as I am, talk as a friend without any hidden agenda to impress my beliefs or practices on another.

But I'm never shy to do the little reminder for people to pray, just in general though. If the person would ask for more details about the topic, then perhaps a little ballroom and breakdance routine might ensue. Who knows, the person might be inclined to try the fancy footwork out, or choose to wait for a better song to dance to. It's all in the timing, the footing, the inner willingness and the dance instructor if there is to be any chance of a person trying out the new dance floor.

Sometimes I wish I could rip a chunk of my heart off and paste it over the spiritual pain that others feel, in the hopes that their heart might beat to another drum. Patience, patience, patience, oh what a word in the human language that plagues me everyday. All I can do is pray that my efforts help in some way, even a micro bit. I can't change the world, I know, but I can sure try!

Chapter 12

What's in the Air with Prayer

Now that I sit here writing this book out, it is obvious to me that I learned Picture Prayers for another important reason; to help increase the frequency of prayer. Without having the luxury of being able to peek into other people's prayers, I can't help but to wonder if people have the same notions I did to ask for the same things over and over again like: Repentance of sins, blessings, forgiveness of others, and help for problems in ones personal life or the world's.

Once, while I was about to start a Picture Prayer, the thought popped into my mind if God liked jokes or not. To me it sure did seem like He had a sense of humor, at least, with all of the odd circumstances I had encountered in my life. Laughter seemed to be a positive emotion which I am certain had to be encouraged by God, yet it wasn't instilled in me to laugh or joke with God. So would it be wrong or disrespectful to do such a thing? Who knew?

So I proposed into my life that in getting personal with God, that I should learn to bring my positive self to the table with Him to learn His likes and dislikes with what He gave me. Humor is a big one for me, because without it I doubt I would keep on ticking. Laughter is just a part of my soul, and I found out that Jesus likes that emotion almost as much as I do. How I know that is a whole other book in itself, literally that I wrote called *Jesus Is No Joke*, when I had some life changing, physically healing and revitalizing visits from Jesus! Now that almost sounded odd for me to even write that down just now, but hey, it's what happened! I can't say Jesus likes jokes in particular, but He has a sparkle in His laughter like no other.

Me and my tangents, now where was I?

I was taught to respect God, receive rewards from God and to do His duty, but I figure that even a solider of God would sit down and make animals out of balloons to see a child smile. In realizing this, there now seems to be a whole new arena of enjoyment for me in getting to know God. It's not that I think it would look very sane of me to be walking around with my head and eyes turned toward the sky, laughing and joking out loud with Him. But now I can stub my toe and roll in agony on the floor and ask God if that was really necessary that I did that just now!

Right when I can make no sense out of something that isn't exactly dire, I can throw up my hands and look God's way in my mind and ask, "Why?" Nothing heavy, just a light joke of my not understanding sent God's way. Yet, I admit there are times when I see something aired on television showcasing one hundred different versions of spiders or something gross where I ask, "Was it really necessary to make more than one kind of ugly spider?" Yeah, I understand that different spiders can only survive in different conditions, but some of them have been hit with the ugly stick once too often to have the mug they do!

I feel God knows I don't mean to be offensive on His creations, because He knows me and the sense of humor He gave me. So far, I don't think that I was a mistake in how I was made so He had to see it coming that I would "go there" about spiders. I now sit and think how cool it is that I can speak pretty freely to God now, without being afraid that I've offended Him.

I do know, however, that there are some limits in approaching God. That good old fashioned tale of having "common sense" when it comes to most anything in life is something I try to apply at all times, even with God. So far, I haven't been told by anyone that I don't have common sense. If anything, I can sometimes appear gullible if people pull that straight face humor on me where I can't tell that the person is joking or not. I try to take people by their word, so I make it appear as if I believe them when they tell me something. Well, I should say that sometimes I'm only halfway paying attention if it sounds like bull to me so I just make the appearance that I go along with it when I've hardly heard a word. Then to hear a quick laugh coming from the tale teller, tells me I've been fooled but at least I have common sense on my side, I think.

I like to think that most people have common sense in what's appropriate in life, and in speaking to God. But I have been stunned to see some reality television moments where people say the wackiest things I have ever seen or heard. One of my favorite reality type moments are when Jay Leno of the Tonight Show, goes and asks simple questions to people on the street like, "Who was the first president of the United States?" Then after some hard pondering, Jay stretches out a dollar bill with the first president's face spread across it and offers it to them if they get it right!

Okay, for some people they might think that's a petty way to confirm common sense or not. But in America it is practically tattooed across our foreheads to know these kinds of basic facts where an eyebrow might be raised if a person didn't know these simple things. Not only have I seen these common sense issues on television but in real life where I know someone who gives me a different answer every time I ask how many states are in the United States. I know, another history question, but if a person lives in the United States and doesn't know this answer they might be a candidate for common sense issues.

I'm not a big fan for laying out rules and regulations where I have no business to, so I don't. My crystal ball is on the fritz, so I also don't know if people in the world are talking to God appropriately or not, either. Yet, I think a lot of people tend to swear, yell or get angry at God.

It happens. Is it appropriate? I think not.

Am I guilty of it? Yes, of course.

Why? I think because I am never going to be perfect and I won't always agree with the decisions God makes. I was angry at God even as a little girl who lost her mother to Him taking her away. What, He didn't know I still needed her? Of course He knew, but He did it anyway. Where was the logic in that decision and how did it help me? I still don't fully understand it, but He did it anyway. I'm sure that's the conversation a lot of people have in their heads when they lose someone close, and I'm no different.

I have heard of some people who lost a loved one and how they got so angry at God that they never wanted to have anything to do with Him, ever again. Like that was really going to show God that He lost a really good person because of what He did. God probably is just sitting there waiting for the resistant person to realize that He takes everyone away at some point. You simply are not going to get out of this life alive (a saying my dad taught me)!

It sucked how I lost my mother, but just like everyone else, she was bound to leave this existence at some point. The timing isn't always the best, but when is it ever? Yet, I know we all have to come into this world and leave this world. I can either go along with God's working plan that's been in motion since the beginning of time here, or pretend it shouldn't happen.

I like to call myself a "stinker" of a sort where I can say that I know that death has to happen, but I won't accept it fully. Meaning, I won't let my life end there by rotting away in a grave as if that is all there is. I know and accept the challenge that I have just a certain amount of time, whatever it may be, for me to get my act straight to find the right button to push that will allow my soul to carry on into another life with God.

I have gotten so angry in the past in seeing innocent children dying by any means and leaving their parents to grieve in heavy despair. I could sometimes feel the pain so vividly I could see how someone would want to turn their back on God, if even for a moment to show their distaste for His decision. But I know now that a crime hasn't been committed by God. If anything, any grieving person should talk to Him about the pain caused and not hold it against Him.

If I got angry at a clockmaker for making the mechanism that allowed me to measure time and know that time was passing me by before I did anything with my life; how would that make sense? God isn't to be held accountable for discontinuing an existence He created in the first place. I know that God set up this world where man, Adam and Eve, could either be blind to death and just hang forever around the Tree of Life or eat of the Tree of Knowledge of good and evil to learn about death and worse things.

That's a pretty easy decision nowadays for anyone who has suffered the loss of a loved one to not want to know death. If it were up to me, I would have chopped down that darn tree to not even have the temptation or eat one of the fruits by accident. To have a serpent or anyone telling me, "C'mon Heidi, jump off the bridge! It's fun to fly, at least for a moment before the splat at the end!" It wouldn't work on me, but it seems someone lacked a little life experience or common sense during the Garden of Eden times. So if there's anyone to be angry at, I say it's due time to point the finger to the appropriate party.

I feel that God allowed man room for growth to learn of even the bad things that can happen in life, and man took a hold of it without regarding the warning. So now, when I think of how terrible death is I know that there was a design in place for something better before that fruit eating incident. I also know that after the knowledge of death comes to us when we die and get that rotten fruit out of our system that was passed down through the generations, that true life comes.

I now try to not get angry at God for the death that comes in this life, but it is hard. I at least don't hold a grudge against Him, and talk to Him about it when it happens. I think the greatest crime that is committed when anyone dies, is if they are not prepared for what happens after their physical death. If that person never knew about the facts of God and Jesus, how would that look when they arrived and were met with Them both? All I can say is I'd hate to be that person!

There are so many different sources out there to learn more about God, that there really are no excuses for people not knowing something about Him and how to act toward Him. I don't feel like any grand resource at the reception desk to God's office or anything and I don't know anyone who really is the source to be had. But if each person who had a little piece of God info were ready to share it at a moments notice, that's a huge source of help. If the topic of God were in the air more or at least felt to be there, more people would feel invited to talk about Him more.

I don't feel I need to wave a giant flag or have a full grown crucifix on my wall at home in every corner to scream out for people to talk to me about God, either. Actions speak louder in showing where my interests are, and how comfortable my spirit is in living how I do. So I like to think that an aroma, aura or an air freshener of invitation to speak to me about God should get the point across. Just something that is absolutely in the air that surrounds me and embraces anyone who meets me to know that I am more than willing to touch on the subject of our Creator with ease and clarity—only if they would like me to, of course.

Chapter 13

Talking Strangers

If I never turned on a radio, television or picked up a newspaper, I don't know how I would ever find out what's going on around me. Okay, so the neighbor next door or my best friend might call me to give me a heads up on the world today. But still, that's just second hand information I would be getting. Perhaps my informative friend missed a detail or two, or simply elaborated on something nonexistent in the facts of the stories being related. If I am not the one getting first hand knowledge, I realize that there's a chance that I won't catch everything meant to be distributed.

As well intended as the neighbor or my friend may be, I know that it's best that I get off my butt and check out the world myself to see what's happening. I feel this is true when it comes to the matter of getting to know God, too. Getting second hand knowledge about God doesn't mean I would be getting the whole picture of what God is about.

Even if I only made half an effort to learn about God or the world around me, there's the chance that I might interpret things wrongly. When the World Trade Center in New York was attacked in 2001 and struck by the first plane, I had turned on the television when the news station was panning out across the city toward the World Trade Center. I hadn't turned up the volume just yet, and from what I could see, New York City was on fire! I just saw billows of smoke pluming over the city, and I thought to myself, "That's one nasty fire going on." Then I turned up the volume, sat down and got more comfortable to learn of the details. The news reporter was already in mid-sentence, rambling on about things I could make no sense of since I came in so late into his report.

So I stuck around as the news station then honed in to another news reporter standing on top of the roof of a nearby building with a shot of the World Trade Center tower clearly on fire in the background. My next thought was, "That's going to be a hard fire to put out being so high up in the building. I wonder how that got started?" Then, the reporter clears it up for me, "It appears that an airplane has accidentally flown into the World Trade Center..." Then while in mid-sentence, the roaring sound of another plane flying low is heard. The reporter takes notice of the plane and watches along with me as it then strikes the next tower and he concludes, "This is no accident..."

Had I not taken more interest to stick around and turn up the volume of my television, I would have thought that New York City was ablaze. My initial impression could have been a lasting one; too, at least until I discovered that nothing else was on television but this tragic event for weeks. I am glad that I did take more initiative and actually tune into the station that caught everything as the tragedy played out and really struck home with me to see it when it happened.

I cannot help but to think where my life would be now had I not taken more interest in the matter of communicating with God. My early experiences in church were nothing less than horribly boring and fear filled. Then my sister Michelle took it upon herself to talk to me and my younger sister about praying. Michelle always took us to church on Sundays during that time, so she knew that we were taught about praying before. But there was something about making the issue of God more personal where He wasn't a stranger to me and in fact had connections to something missing in my life at the time; my mother.

Well, that helped!

God wasn't just in a building where a man who dressed in robes spoke loud using big words, making me sit still with an authoritative voice when he called for prayer. God became someone that knew me, my mother, my dogs and then became an ever present comforter.

Had I just suffered through the church sermons in my childhood where I never looked back and just treated it all like something I just *had* to do, would I be the same person? I can't lie; I really haven't attended church regularly since I wasn't made to after the age of 18 and moved out on my own. I also can't say that I think of my time in church sermons having been fully worthwhile since I cannot recall ever really paying attention to most of them. But I can say that I am glad to have gone through the experience where it made me want to seek out more.

There are a lot of people passionate about God and do have good information to share, but it's a whole other experience to bring the God experience home. Each of my pastors just glowed of good intentions and did their best to encourage other people to know God. Hmm, in thinking on it now, their preaching worked! I personally didn't like to get preached to, but preferred instead to go within myself and seek out information to know God better. I'm sure for other people that attending sermons helps their understanding, and I understand that can be helpful being that I have felt it necessary to give a lecture or two myself. Anything that brings God closer and motivates people to accept and receive answers related to God; is a positive.

At some point, the biggest question that seems to grace the mind of most people that concerns them and God is, "What is the meaning of my life?" I could hardly imagine that I would even get a glimpse at my own purpose had I not gotten to know God as I have. If I were estranged from God, it would be one wild life of shooting around ideas about what my life lessons meant.

In taking a moment to pause and think about that concept just now, I got a whole rambling of oddities in my head about what it would be like to live without acknowledging God in my life. I love making crazy lists of emotions to express myself, so I'm going to have a go at creating one now:

Life without God would be a life of aimless, meaningless, stubbing my toe in the dark, empty, wasteful, joy lacking, kicking my heart across the floor with lint clinging to it in clumps, putting my shoes on the wrong feet every morning, dingy, worn-out young, leaving dirty diapers to ferment on my pillow each night, I can't read that fine print at the bottom of my soul wrapper and where's the expiration date on this label anyhow!

Just a smidgen of confusion would be had in my life where I would probably think a lot about what my purpose was without God, too. I mean really, it's not like God just gave me a spreadsheet of what my life was to entail. I had to do some feeling around on my own to discover what it was I was going to do with my life. In knowing God and getting these little hints and visions along the way, really let me know I was on the right track.

But, (and that's a huge "but") I am not perfect!

At times even I know that I forget where my place is in what I feel I am to be doing in this lifetime. My human mind is a wanderer; it likes to focus on one thing at a time or a ton of things at once. I don't know whether I'm coming or going when I drift off into my little world of concerns. It's like having a little ant farm in my hands where a nest of ants are pressed between two pieces of glass and live their lives out for me to focus on. I could watch for hours and follow the struggle of one little ant to reach the surface of the mud packed between the glass, without my having looked outside of the ant farm all of that time.

I know that I do that in life where I let myself get lost in the moment of the struggle at hand and I forget to look outside of it to see that God is just waiting for me to glance His way. Even in learning Picture Prayers, as fast and simple as it is for me now, I can lose perspective. It's odd because I do feel as if my head and heart is always open to conversing with God, but darn it all if I don't act human and look inside my ant farm too long!

It kind of makes me laugh when I do that ant farm focus and realize it later on. Because I know what it would look like if I was sitting in my office waiting for a therapy session, for example, only to see my patient staring at an ant farm in the next room and keep me waiting. I would wonder what the big deal was with that little ant farm held so tightly in his hands. I can only imagine the look on God's face in seeing me in the same situation being so concerned about something so minor in life that I forgot to even chat with Him about my ant farm of an issue!

Treating God like a stranger to my life is a strange deed to do, as if this is a life I fully control. Consciously, I've made God a big part of my life in all that I do and think of. It's such a consistent thing for me to think of doing the right thing in my own eyes, which doesn't always look for an outright approval from God but more of a, "I do this because I am on the same side for good which is God's way." Yet, I flub and fumble and forget to even bring the main course of me to the table of God to help serve up the dinner!

Man, I'm weird with my analogies!

Incorporating God into my life more fully is a process I think most people struggle to do, and it's to be expected. Again, I know God made me the way I am and I try my best, which is all I can do. God is no stranger to me, so I can and do get firsthand knowledge of what and who He is. Most importantly, the word "stranger" is a word meant for people I don't know, only, and God is a wonder that knew me from my beginning where I was never a stranger to Him.

Chapter 14

My Wireless Carrier

If I put individual religious beliefs to the side, I know that prayers in some form are universally good and practiced by most religions. Getting caught up in how people should and should not pray, or practice their beliefs, has never been a goal or effort of mine. I have always found it more intriguing to look at how similar faiths are, and how individual needs are made known through deep thought and projecting those thoughts.

Cutting corners in any fashion while in prayer is also not a goal behind what it means for me to do Picture Prayers. Getting myself and others to pray more and add more positive intentions in the world and toward God, however, are the goals. Praying in the manner that I have learned gives me an expressive and active communication with the source of all things that are good, in one instant of focus. Saying that Picture Prayers is better than what has been taught to me in the tradition of my Christian beliefs isn't even regarded, only that every little bit of prayer helps us all in this world of God's.

Praying can be such a private matter where there can be no telling if a person participates in it or not. In having the ability to be so discreet while in prayer shows me that praying creates a freedom that can be had in any part of the world under any circumstance. There just are no strings attached to me that will indicate to the world, "Heidi is in prayer mode now—so please watch your step!"

Chances are that no one reading these pages has any strings attached to them either, aside from intravenous lines and an occasional handcuffing or shackle. Yet and still that means no one can order you or me to be obedient to believe in a certain way, even if we are impressed upon to actually go through the *motions* of prayer—doesn't mean we are actually going through the *emotions* of any of it. Not that any uprising should be had or encouraged, but even with those handcuffed readers there's a real freedom within that no one can force when it comes to prayer.

I respect the ideas of tradition and the thoughts garnered towards an individual's faith being thought of as the best and only blessed way of doing things. I don't always agree or even understand all of what people believe these days, but I stand firm, to be tolerant of other's beliefs and related habits as long as they don't hurt another. I know some people might overly concern themselves to pick at such a topic and say, "Yeah, but what about those people who do this or that. Do you agree to let that kind of stuff slide?"

Personally, as an individual, I don't think I have that much pull to convince many people to "slide" in one direction over another. In all honesty, I don't think my opinion matters that much in the world of religion. I think enough conflict; war and hate have been nurtured along to a full enough blossom where I don't care to add any more poop to the soil for that sort of thing to grow.

Prayer and religion, I believe, are two different things. When I pray to God, I don't identify myself and rank. "Hey there God, Heidi here from the Midwest, 8th row pew sitter in church (I liked to hide back there), of the Christian faith…calling on you for the following…" I simply doubt my prayer would be directed to a different section of God's ear if I pointed out my location or angle of belief to Him prior to beginning my prayer.

It all sounds kind of funny to me, but you know what, I think somewhere inside of me at some point, I thought I was a prime praying person. I mean, I'm me, and I know I'm a decent person who wouldn't aim to talk to God wrongly. So if anyone else was praying in a manner that wasn't what I was doing, heck, they must be doing something wrong. I think it's logical to an extent to feel that way, and a lot of folks can find a Bible quote to back up why they do what they do just to add to why their way is best.

But here comes another "you know what," I know now that it's not about being better than the other person or trying to call a tradition or faith wrong. For me, today, and all of my writing-ramblings, still all I aim to do is make more praying happen!

I feel like a proud rooster cock-a-doodling on my post to make sure all the other poultry heard my urgent cries or something!

How in the heck did I get here and where was I? Ah…I was talking about prayers, I think.

As I see it, praying doesn't happen enough or there would be a lot less garbage seen floating down our drainage ditches of reason today. There's no science or polls that need to be taken, just an ear to the ground will suffice to hear the rumbles of discontent in the world. Go ahead, get on your knees to take a listen, I'll be patient and wait…

If I were to doodle out on my post to encourage prayer and say it's best to make prayer more convenient, some people might envision a drive-thru to prayer. Then I'd get those "nothing good comes easy" speeches, and that conversations with God are not to be rushed. If I say that prayer needs to be simplified, people might think that I mean keep it simple, don't mention compli-cating things to God.

Without any frills or confusion, the simplest way to put it is, "We need to pray more, people!"

Whatever it takes to get to that point of upping the prayer

quota in the world seems to be the magical key to unity. Thoughts transgress language, culture, color, nationalities, limbo competitions, and even square dancing. Like a mist of lava, if there ever were such a thing, it singed into my brain that prayer can encourage harmony even among people. That is, if the prayers are for common sense goodness.

In prayer for goodness, there is no war or hate. Minds pointed to positive prayers can't lift an arm to aim a rifle at someone's head, or scream profanities at a passerby. In my soul's eye, prayer is absolutely necessary to be brought to the forefront of everyone's mind. The world needs prayer in order to survive, it's not an option and there is no time to waste on considering praying or not.

It's almost weird to think that some people actually don't even think to pray as if they are the only ones who can hear their thoughts. Imagine a clairvoyant following you around all day, just a step behind or ahead of you saying, "I heard that!" Wouldn't you be more mindful on what you thought of? Maybe it would help to put a better title instead of some "anonymous clairvoyant" and call this step-a-header *"The All Supreme Creator."* Feel like clearing up your ambitious thoughts now?

Thinking of prayer in this manner helped me to know more of the nature of the communication that I already had with God, whether I knew or acknowledged it. I didn't even have to assume a position or aim my brain toward anything to *try* to talk with God. He was already hearing me loud and clear, and to even think of some of the times when He entered and answered some of my most private thoughts—well that just clears any doubts I would have of His listening skills.

I didn't always think of God and deep down I didn't know what the heck it truly meant to chat with Him. I also tended to wane a bit at different times in my life, on the importance of the act of praying and how consistent I was with it. Yet, there was always a bit of prayer in my life, just enough to keep my mind and heart open.

For various reasons, a unique package of prayer was dropped on my front porch to open up and bring into my life. I would like to think of it as a mystery package, if only for a moment I could play dumb and not see the full necessity of prayer. Sadly, I do sometimes look to the lives of other people and wish I could be blind like some of them are to any expectations from God. It's not a terribly heavy burden or anything; it would just be "neat" in a sense to be clueless and to just "be". But if that was all I was meant to do in this life is "be" I suppose I could have been born as a rock and proved God proud that I lived my life as expected. With only a toe or two resembling anything like a rock, I suppose I'm expected to have a bit more "oomph" (i.e. effort put forward) in this lifetime and pay a little homage to the Man above.

I know now that reverence for God can come in various forms, and even in a form that I could have never dreamt up myself with Picture Prayers. I'm sure there are other prayer methods already out there that I've never heard of that would add to my prayer knowledge, as well. But now that I have a glimpse of how wonderful, beautiful and natural prayer can be, I can't help but to think of what I can compare it to.

With cellular phones keeping us in touch wherever we are, and helping out in all sorts of emergencies and issues; prayers in the way I have now learned could be looked at as the supreme cell phone of all! If I could develop a special cell phone I would call it the Picture Perfect Prayer Phone. Ah yes, I am lighting a match to my imagination once again ☺:

Okay, so first, the Prayer Phone itself would be free with no other purchase necessary or coupons required and no time limitation on the free phone offer.

In addition, there would be no need for worrying about your minutes of prayer being used wisely or only for emergencies. So few minutes would be needed anyways to get your message across with Picture Praying that there would also be no overage charges. In fact, since the Prayer Phone is for *such* a good cause and God would lend His time freely to take all calls; all phone calls would in fact be ultimately free!

Is this a bargain or what?

Hmm, it kind of gives me the thought that I should start placing some Prayer Phones out on the corners for people to practice with. I wouldn't even have to have batteries or a line hooked up to them since God can pick up a whisper clear across the galaxy. Place the phone, leave it, and put instructions for each person to leave it for others to give it a try. As long as it gets people to dedicate more time to prayer, I'm game; mission accomplished!

Now I'm wondering if anyone will give me a call and ask if they can help me build some Prayer Phones to distribute. That's a phone call I'll gladly take myself!

Chapter 15

God's too Busy to Hear Me

The pity prayer parties are out there and I know about them because I've thrown a few of those parties myself. It's those talks with yourself where you say things like, "Why would God want to listen to me and my stinking problems anyway?" Then there's: "Who knows if God will even think that I deserve to have Him answer my prayers?"

I would feel like there were worse things going on in the world than my little trip over the curb that twisted my ankle, or the friend who wouldn't return phone calls, so why bother God about it? I sometimes thought that since God had a billion and one things to do in His day, that if I came to His front door to ask about something it had better be a rehearsed prayer (so He wouldn't have to listen too hard) or something darn important!

In looking through the Bible as an adult now, and putting in a search with my CD ROM Bible program, I could find no trace of there being a limit to prayers. Yet, I couldn't figure out why I had it in me to be hard on myself in what I could or should pray about. From what I could gather, it wasn't even an instilled notion in me to be that way, only that I wanted to respect God and value His time the way I valued my own.

I knew I didn't always have the time to sit and listen to my friend's problems at all times of day or night. I had a job to go to, bills to mail out, gas to pump, shopping to do, a remote control to my television to find and to seek out my eyeglasses to see any of it! Of course I made time for chatting with my friends sometime between finishing the errands and my first anticipated television program to watch in the evening. Then when the programs would come on, I suddenly didn't hear my phone anymore or think that if it was important the person calling would leave a message for me to get back to them. So, I do have some set of priorities in my head about how responsible I should be for the necessities in my life and being there for friends. Yet, I know that I am never quite up to where I should be in the world outside of my own head and needs.

I figured that here I am a single person in a maze of people with things to do everyday, so God must surely have priorities of His own. I could imagine someone hanging over a cliff with their safety rope having failed them while scaling a mountain and them crying for help to God. This kind of situation is a tad bit dire and urgent. God would certainly have to run over as fast as He could to see what the situation may be and if His help should be applied or to allow that person to join Him in the next life.

Then there's me. "God, do you think I should buy this used car with the new CD player in it, or the car without any rust that doesn't even have a radio installed?"

What a silly thing to ask about when I knew somewhere in the world God was making a life or death decision and here I wanted to know about a car choice! I had better just say my rehearsed prayer and hope God could sense my dilemma, so I won't feel guilty for asking.

Guilt, shame, embarrassment, and bashful ideas came into my head before I would consider asking God about minor incidences in my life. Well, in comparison to life and death situations, I felt my issues were minor anyhow. Heck, even hospitals had the habit of taking more seriously injured patients before the person who just needed a splinter taken out of their foot. There just is an assumed hierarchy of importance instilled in the world around us all that brings this sort of thinking to the forefront.

Then by some grace of God I fell off the wagon of ridiculousness and allowed some oxygen to seep into my newly cracked skull. I got to thinking, "Hey, buying a car is a big deal to me even if it doesn't look like it from afar. God knows what this means to me."

I began to realize that it was okay to mention in my prayers about the little things going on in my life. I did it to some extent anyhow from the beginning, I just didn't elaborate on what I was saying. But learning to talk to God with more detail, as I would my friends, taught me a lot. I would like to think that I value God more than I do my friends, and that He is at least to be considered one of my best friends of all time. So why exclude Him out of my daily thoughts and needs, no matter how minor?

If God had a routine of creating new creatures to inhabit other planets at noon, or make our oceans deeper in certain spots at midnight; He never gave me a word of complaint about talking to Him at these times. I also saw no lightning strikes nearby; not even static electricity in the air to let me know that God didn't appreciate my topic of prayer choice, either. God was just there in some manner of the word, taking account of my prayer and even lending some hints for answers.

It became where it wasn't okay anymore to think that it was acceptable for someone in my mental world to push me to the side to speak their prayer before mine. There was no taking turns on the playground of life to be sure everyone got a spin on the prayer ride. Instead it was up to each person to speak their part to God, and know that He could handle them all.

My placing a human attribute to God as if He had no time for my odd thoughts or issues, proved to be a silly mistake. It was a dark alley that no one should go down because I can swear to having found nothing but potholes of misjudgment on my part. I now more fully realize that God is infinitely capable to take on all the billions of us on this planet, at once. If He were incapable to handle all of us, why on Earth would He have created us all?

If I had a glass tank of hamsters, and allowed them to mate continuously and create new baby hamsters, I admit that I wouldn't be able to handle them all at once. My solution would then be to not allow them to mate so much to keep their numbers low enough for me to take care of them. I'm no god, but to the hamsters, I sure could control them enough to be fewer in numbers where I still could manage them.

God hasn't placed any limits on the number of people who can live upon this Earth. I figure if there were too many people where we were getting out from under God's control, He wouldn't allow for us all to keep being born. Unlike myself who might also consider giving away some of the hamsters if their numbers got out of control, God wouldn't do this either.

God instead says there is room and time for everyone on Earth and in Heaven. Unlimited; God is simply immeasurable in being able to see to all of our needs. It's only when I look to what I would do with actual or possible instances in my own life, as in the thought of having mating hamsters, do I see the bigger picture.

Sometimes my thoughts and made up scenarios even make me laugh, but it really simplifies the world around me and my questions about God. It puzzles me where all of these scenarios come from, because sometimes they sound too good to even have come from my own head. Then I remember how the greatest Teacher of the Bible spoke in parables, which are stories that relate to everyday life to explain a point about God. That Teacher was Jesus. Who better is there to follow as an example to relate God's intentions?

I personally enjoy the way that Jesus got His points across without putting fluffy words to explain things away. Instead He took a simple matter met in life and used it as a means to convey what was needed. Without my adding a bit of rationality of everyday life into the formula of my God communications and understandings I think I would still be contemplating the very first level of my prayers.

I find it's important that if there is to be any growth in my understanding of God's capacity to hear me and hear me good, I can always rely on my God given common sense. There are a lot of guidelines and pointers that help out along the way, too. But I know if I truly sit down on a soft patch of grass, with quiet all around, that I am complete with what God has given me to feel His intentions:

He hears me.
He sees me.
He knows me.
He guides me.
He loves me.

There aren't any riddles, or pecking order in the way of my reaching out to God. I should have always felt and known these simple truths, but this physical world can really screw with a person's head to forget what's really important and known. I'm certain that I'll forget these points again at some point, only to revisit them later, as always. It's like clockwork now to know I'll just wander off in my own thoughts and forget that God is watching and willing. Flaws are sometimes fun to work with, and even more of a thigh slapping laugh when I remember that I figured this issue out already.

I'm sure God saw this all coming with my missteps and assumptions being all cockeyed at odd hours. It's good to know He's there, and has the time to wait for me to come around again. I just hope that I keep a steady head on these human attributes I often beam God's way. After writing a whole chapter on it, one would think I could hold it in my head always to know I'm just as important as the next person with my prayers. But it's not so bad to be polite to allow another's prayer ahead of mine at times, is it?

There I go again God.

Chapter 16

No Quotes: A Chapter of Prayers

With so much structure in the world today and with so many people often seeking that structure where they feel compelled to ask this very question about anything new they learn: "Am I doing it right?" I dedicate this chapter to them. Like I've said before, I had always looked for someone to point me in the direction of a better or even best way to pray. Millions if not billions of people prayed every day, so there had to be someone out there who knew what was best.

To say that I know best, or I know anything at all is not even something I debate in my head. All I know is that I am comfortable in the way that I pray and if that works for someone else, then so be it.

But I know how eager I was to learn and even follow the manner in which others prayed, so I thought I would take a look at my prayers typed out to see how they looked on paper. I also thought it to be a good idea just in case anyone would like to follow along just to be sure they knew where I was coming from:

Prayer 1:

"

In Jesus' name.
Amen.

Prayer 2:
"

"

In Jesus' name.
Amen.

And we can't forget:
Prayer 3:

"

"

In Jesus' name.
Amen.

Any questions? I suggest everyone to feel free to share these prayers with anyone who will listen and fill in the blanks for themselves.

In all honesty, I really do feel like just leaving the chapter as this. It would make more sense for me to do that than for me to fill in the blanks to form prayers for mere strangers and their unknown lives. When people asked me what my next book was about while I was writing this book I would just simply say it was about praying. Automatically people assumed I was just writing out prayers that people should say and how they should say them. I didn't want to elaborate on what I was writing just yet, because I'd had instances where I shared something I was writing about and it came back to me in print or even published, or where what I said was even told to me as a taught lesson as if I'd never heard it before! I'm a great believer in there being a time and place for everything, and that usually is when the person who is meant to share does it in the manner that God intended.

So, I kept the main meat of this book to myself, although I had shared parts before about praying in pictures with a handful of people and yes—even one put a bit of it in print ☺! To an extent, some of those people might have guessed what I might incorporate into this book. But the questions kept coming, and then the questions changed in a direction that surprised me. Those that didn't know me very well would say, "Oh a book on praying; you must be really religious then!"

I could see the idea of praying having an inkling of a connection to religious thoughts and practices, but when the assumption was posed to me it always stunned me a bit. I would of course give a quick reply of "no" and it wasn't as if it was an insult, yet something was distasteful about it all.

Again, in my head I would visualize the inside of formal churches, formal clothes, and perfect manners that all spelled out my childhood Sundays. I, of course, thought maybe this was where the distaste came from once again. Then it came to me that possibly the thought of being a person who placed limits and formalities on approaching God, brought the sour taste in my mouth with this "religious" assumption. I have already gone through having the common sense in being respectful in approaching God, so this wasn't a part of my issue in being formal in regard to God.

Praying for me has always been a free spirited event, where I wasn't needing to be directly involved with a religion to practice prayer. It always struck me as funny to get those kinds of remarks, and there always seemed to be a look of surprise from the assumer when I told them I wasn't very religious. Then I'd follow it up with a slightly questioning look without being able to control myself from doing so. Then I'd see resolve come over their face as if they just thought I was a person who wrote poetry in prayer form. I can't be certain this was the case, but when no more questions came forward I also had to make my assumptions.

If they only knew that my little "prayer poems" would include only quotation marks with blank spaces in-between them. For the people that knew me better and asked about the new book I was writing, I would be brief again and just say it was about prayers. Then I'd usually get an "Oh, Lord!" sort of response out of them, sometimes literally they would say this. It was more of a, "God only knows how you are going to handle that topic!" and "What kind of trouble are you going to get yourself into now?" All blended into one little phrase.

They knew and I knew whatever it was I would be up to in this book that it wouldn't be the usual and nothing close to being prayer poems. I kind of liked that I had that effect on the people who knew me; because they knew that I wouldn't want to "reinvent the wheel". If there was something out there that had the information I was looking for when I needed it, I surely wouldn't have sat on my buttocks this long to repeat and write the same old story. It gets too painful to have any time for that.

I'm happy to say that I won't be putting any prayers in this book to have people repeat after me. If I knew I had perfection going on in my prayers, then I would have a different attitude. Now when people ask me how I pray, what to pray and all that prayer stuff, I tell them to do what comes natural. Fill in the blanks, go sideways, back and forth or in circles; say whatever it takes to fulfill your heart in communicating with God. Each of us knows our lives best and what needs God given attention, so "go there!"

Chapter 17

Essence of Time

With the always impending doom of there being an end to this world, or at least the end to our own lives, I figure that it makes sense for anyone to act now with prayer while they are still able to. Even with negative reports of things happening in the world today that should prompt some concern to try to make things better, or at least to hope for it. I personally like to think of human beings as being hopeful creatures, anyhow.

We hope for independence, for more money, a nicer house, new clothes, a classic, 1970 Corvette Stingray painted in sparkling-purple (okay—so that's my personal hope), a cheap babysitter; we all hope for something. But I wondered how often we hope for things like this or basic essentials for the mere survival of other occupants in this world? Whenever I drift off into my world of wants and needs, my goal is to always try to spot someone in the news or elsewhere who could use what I already owned and find contentment with what I possessed.

Here I start to get picky and wanting better, when the sky opens up wider for me to see the Sun peering down on me where suddenly nothing I own in this world really matters. I start to think about God, Heaven, Jesus, the afterlife and how I can be certain that I am doing the right things in this life to be closer to God. Once the clouds pass over and block out this sunny enlightenment, this is when I finally look back down to the stuff I have and wonder how I accumulated so much junk and why it once seemed so important to have it all!

In relocating for a bit to Melbourne, Victoria, I realized quickly that I had to downsize what I owned. There was no way I could take it all with me nor keep everything and absolutely enjoy every bit of what I owned where it deserved to remain sitting stored in a corner or a sealed box. While rummaging through what I owned I discovered various items, even some that I had since childhood. Memories of fun times came forward in my mind invoked by some of the items in front of me. There was so much attached to what I was seeing, where these items served great purposes for me at some point.

While I reminisced and totally got off track in what I was doing, I began to realize something about these items in front of me: The thrill was gone! In other words, these items had already served their purpose for me at a certain time in my life, whether it was during my childhood or last year.

I now had new adventures to take on in a different country, and lugging all of my stuff around just wasn't going to happen. There were others out there who could benefit from the things that had once brought me great joy, so I ended up donating a great amount of my things to charity. I admit that some of it was hard to let go of, but knowing that they would eventually help another let me know that I was spreading some of my own personal joy in some way.

It was a good learning experience for me in having to let go of physical items that were perfectly fine, but I knew had already reached their peak in pleasing me. I now realize that this life is much the same in learning how to value my physical life for what it is and what it brings. It isn't about accumulating wealth and items to only allow for me to enjoy them, but to see that once I was done enjoying what God provided me with to allow others to enjoy it, too.

I wasn't independently wealthy where I hadn't sold some items in the process on my own for my Australia move, but I was able to still give a part of myself along with my worldly possessions. Some people are greater than I can be in this lifetime to give away all that they own, but I truly believe it is reasonable to appreciate and personally make use of what God gives us in this lifetime. When the time has come for those items to benefit another, no matter how luxurious, then so be it.

Logically and reasonably, not everything can be lugged around in my life and not everything can be sold and turned into cash. Besides, it feels so much better inside to give when it's done for the direct benefit of others instead of in a forced situation. A forced situation is much like someone who might die before they believe it is their time. There's so much wealth attained in a lifetime in so many tiny and other larger, more noticeable ways. If I died now I would look to all of my little and larger assets that I recently hadn't used and just wished I'd had the chance to give it to the right person who could truly use and value it.

I know that I'll never be perfect and will always have extra items to spare, but I make an effort to try harder now to not have so much excess. I never know when my time might be up in this lifetime, so I know I need to keep this sort of thinking always working in my life. It goes without saying, as well, in regards to my praying habits.

As it's mentioned in the title of this chapter, time is of the essence in a lot of ways. I realize that the very planet that humans reside on is a fragile creature, where prophetic writings of visionaries and prophets predict the cataclysmic end to us all. The question is always, "When will this 'end' all take place?" Then there's the hidden question, "Should I get ready for it now, or later?"

Just like lugging around a ton of things I didn't use for long periods of time, it was a huge challenge to sort it all out at the last minute before my big move to Melbourne. It would have been a cinch if I had always been mindful enough to get rid of or give away items throughout my life at a regular rate. But of course, I had some odd sense in me that I could always deal with it at a later time, or even perhaps take it all with me wherever I went.

Whether it's the end of the world or just the end of one lifetime, I don't think anyone would want to try to clean out a lifetime of skeletons out of their closet in their last breath. Besides, that could be one huge closet space needing to be cleared! I've often thought about how my last moments of life will be, as odd or as common as that might sound. I've wondered if I'll have a painful death, a long drawn out death, or an, "Oops, I just slipped out of my body without noticing it" death.

If it was to be a painful death like tumbling down a mountain side on my roller blades, I wondered what my thoughts would be. I would probably feel a bit stunned as I tumbled, crying out to God the whole way down, knowing me. If I were still conscious upon reaching the bottom, I think I would really put my best effort forward to be sure my sins were forgiven. Then I'd hope God would accept me if it were my apparent time to go to Him. So much effort would have to be expelled in my last ditch effort after a lifetime of work to reach God. Because of this lifetime work, I would know God heard me, and know His limitations, and have an idea of what to expect as I crossed over to the other side.

I could hardly imagine someone who had never considered much of their soul's worth to God up until that last moment, what kind of desperation would be felt when they realized their essence was moving on after their physical death. It would have to be a scary feeling of truly going on into the unknown that they hadn't bothered to look into. Yet, it seems when people are in need the most, whether a believer or not, that phrase, "Help me God!" Always seems to pass over lips. I am certain it is always heard by

Him, too, and He wouldn't ignore it.

If I were to die a long death like dying from a disorder or cancer, there are all sorts of stages of coming to terms with such a death sentence. Having a long time to ponder the physical end to one's existence, I am certain at some point that I would try to right the wrongs I'd done in my life. I think that I would also look more into the miracles and stories that proved more to the existence of the soul and its adventures to the other side. Prayer would be an essential routine, most especially in knowing that it helped to prepare my soul for what's to come for me in the near future. I would aim to be pristine and fully ready for when my day of departure happened to put my mind at ease and those who loved me. Even being a person who feels close to God with prayer always nearby, there's always room for improvement to prepare for my souls' next adventure.

I've heard of people who are dying of any variety of diseases who get angry with God and choose to not get closer to Him as if that is admitting defeat to the disease. I would never think of the gift of life not being worth fighting for, but during the fight there's room for God, too. Turning ones back to God not only hurts them, but God and anyone concerned about the well being of the person's soul.

With the sudden "I slept too soundly with my face in my pillow and died in my sleep" sort of death, things could be interesting with a sudden soul slippage like that. If I didn't know any better about God, I wonder how I would react to finding myself outside of my body heading for who knows where! Even knowing about God and the afterlife, I think if I went to bed and suddenly found myself being met with the Creator, an element of shock would still be in the air with me! There's no last minute, "God forgive me's" or long ponderings on which way to approach God. It's all done, curtains are closed for my act of life, and it's just me and Him now.

I wonder how many people have been met with that sort of

end of life surprise, and how well prepared they were and why they had no last minute chances given. In hearing about so many heart attacks, strokes, and deadly accidents in the world today, it seems there are a lot of people who don't get to have the last say in this lifetime about their soul purposes. Seems to me then that it should be a priority to make an example of ones life, and let it speak for us if we are not able to.

Sometimes, for weirdness' sake, I look into the eyes of the people who surround me on this planet and kind of say to myself, "We are all in this together where we are all going to die someday—but on an individual basis." Not one of us is going to cheat death, it's going to happen, and the more we live the sooner that day of dying will come. It almost seems too dreadful to think about, but it's like a chore of life:

"Hello world, yep, I'm born now."

"I'm potty trained now."

"I can ride a bike, and now drive a car."

"I go to work everyday, and sometimes to church on Sundays."

"I met a lady, fell in love and asked her father if I could marry her."

"Now I like watching sports on television, fusing with the wife, getting the kids off to school and oops...I died now!"

It just kind of happens, unplanned, unrehearsed and many times at unexpected moments in the darndest places. Funerals get planned, our dead bodies get stuffed with chemicals and are sobbed over, our husk gets thrown in the ground and our souls move on even if our loved ones hold on to our memories for their entire lifetime. No one gets used to this process, and yet the process continues as it always has, even if we deny it in our own lives by not preparing for it.

How strange it is for me to think of my not existing as I do on this Earth; moving, dancing, remote controlling, reading, hanging with friends, and laughing. I cannot even fathom the thought, but in being realistic, some time needs to be given to this unavoidable conclusion to my time here. Praying helps me with this acceptance of my physical demise.

There is no magic potion, plastic surgery or remedy to stop nature, but the soul is magic in itself. It doesn't end when the physical body dies, there's nothing like it and whether it gets acknowledged or not—properly, it will take the part that is "you" to another place. I just prefer to help inspire my soul to go back from whence it came, some call it God's House or Heaven, I just like to call it Home.

Chapter 18

An Exercise in Prayer

After going on and on about my life adventures into praying and sharing how important I feel it is to pray regularly, I don't think this book is complete without talking directly. Throughout what I've written here is much the same way I would share parts of my life and concerns with my friends or family. That's why there's little fancy talk or big words written here, because I like to "keep it real" and personable.

Though, even when talking to friends about me and my concerns, I always throw in a, "Ya know what I'm saying?" Just to be sure that I'm clear and not just rambling on without them catching my meaning of the conversation. Since we're all friends here now; and you, the reader, have really gotten to know me in my praying sense of the word, I figured why not talk to you directly for once. It's about time anyhow since I think this book is nearly done from where I'm sitting.

There are probably a million thoughts floating through some of your heads about attempting Picture Prayers, like what angle you should take and why. So I figured I would propose an exercise to you to see if we are indeed on the same page here with some of your thoughts concerning praying in pictures. So, do me a favor and grab a photo album hanging around your house or find a folder on your computer full of pictures, if you can.

Now, before you open it, try to write everything down on a paper to express what you anticipate is inside the album or folder. Heck, I'll make it easy for you. Try to describe just one anticipated picture inside, down on the paper. Make sure you don't miss anything. I want to know about the colors, the smiles, the laughter, the atmosphere and all that goes into that one picture and what was going on in it.

It takes a lot of space to get that down, doesn't it? Feel free to grab some more paper. I have a lot of time on my hands here.

Now open the photo album or folder, and find that picture you thought was in there and see if you missed anything. Did you miss the fragrance in the air, the silly face someone was making, or the piece of dog hair stuck to your lip? Most likely, you forgot to write something down where the full essence wasn't captured with your words written on paper.

With this simple exercise it's possible to see the angle you can take in capturing the full essence of a moment in your life, it's much like taking a snapshot in time. Of course there's no guarantee that any one of us will get every detail right during moments of our life by going on our memory alone. Even if I let you cheat a little, and let you look at a photo for over an hour, you can bet you won't get all of the details of the moment right. For this very reason is why I feel it's necessary that we all feel free to pray when the moment of needed prayer happens, as it happens. Details will be missed otherwise, and the sooner prayer happens the sooner God will respond.

Another aspect clearly seen in this little exercise is something that I quoted earlier when the angelic presence taught me Picture Prayers: "Words fall short of what is meant." You could fill a page or more of what you thought was in one picture of your photo album and still not get all of the details written down fully. How easy of an exercise it is to see that our life of concerns goes further than formulated words.

Let's try another little exercise to see how to flex our Picture Prayer muscles. We know the principles; prayers are from the heart, not the head. The words we use in prayer are good guides, but in time, it seems that we will not have to rely on them as much. As with anything, practice makes perfect in trying to pray in pictures.

So pick a target, like I don't know, an old woman you know who lives alone and struggles to keep up with her home on her own. See her in your mind, walking up her porch steps carrying in heavy groceries and you think without words how you hope she finds a way through her days. Now see yourself running up and carrying her groceries in for her and volunteering to do some chores for her in your spare time. Hey, I said we all need to pray more, I didn't say anything about being lazy!

With good intentions should come action, too. To sit back and pray that someone will help the old woman who you could help yourself in your own way, sends messages—don't you think? This goes for a lot of things that we place into our prayers, but could help with in some small way.

Oh, I feel a list coming on and I don't think it's going to be a pretty one. I don't mean to offend anyone, but these are some of the things I observe in the world on a larger scale that make me scratch my head over and over again and wonder why more doesn't get done when we can all see these things occurring around us:

Prayer vs. Action:

There's praying that no one will feel the need to lock their car door when driving through a poorer neighborhood, when there are groups a person can get involved with that could encourage change in those areas through various conjoined efforts via the community.

There's praying that no one will feel any amount of racial tension, when there are ways to reach out one-on-one or widespread to speak to communities about racial tensions to give them a new face (our own) to relate to about this problem.

There's praying that children in foster care will find a home, while we watch as some go to great lengths to adopt children from across the globe while children just down the road go without gaining a loving family. Perhaps some encouragement can be inspired into those we know looking for children, to adopt with less requirements.

There's praying for the wrongdoings felt to be done by our world governments, when more effort could be placed by every individual to see to it that the people's voices whom our governments are employed by, are indeed heard for critical decisions.

There's praying that people in this world will learn to love one another, and treat their neighbor as they would their own family, when even we as individuals find it hard to forgive a family member for a single mistake.

These are seemingly bigger than one individual prayers of action, but individuals create movement and the change needed as needed. Any effort, no matter how small can go a long way. From one email, to a You Tube phenomena, one never knows where their words may lead.

Still, a lot goes into having the heart to pray for change, especially if we can be a part of that change. It's not that we shouldn't ask at all then, but we should think about what we are asking for and see if we can be of help. I often think about what I'm doing here, if I'm on the right track and if there's something more I could do to help with my prayer movement. Hmm, I guess I do sort of think of what I'm aiming for is a 'movement' since it is a change in attitude with prayer. Praying in pictures is how I really shifted my mind-set in my focus, involvement and broadness on what to approach God with.

There's so much more depth that can be reached by praying with what we live everyday in our visual world. Yet, it's not exclusively about just being able to visualize things, but to make use of our hearts and emotions. Visuals can help guide our prayer thoughts, but without the emotion behind it then it is very much like a plain photo that doesn't strike a person in any way.

In other words, if I'm looking at a Christmas photo from when I was a kid, I'm able to tell you what toy I got, how happy it made me, which sister wanted what I got, and how pretty I thought the wrapping paper was! I know how this time made me feel, even when I didn't voice what I thought of the wrapping paper or how my sister shot daggers out of her eyes for my toy. Some things go without saying, but my emotional connection to the events tells it all.

Actually, a real photo can truly be a helpful guide to how we feel individually about given occurrences in our lives. If I had a photo of a person who did me wrongly and I had a hard time forgiving them, I might keep a photo nearby to address in my prayers of hopes. For me, if something is out of sight, it can often slip my mind. So I'm all for keeping reminders close to keep concerns fresh in my heart to address in my prayers.

I can sometimes take things a step further and keep a magazine or newspaper clipping close to my bed for my more continued prayers for a predicament needing more than a one time prayer. I haven't tried this myself, but I always thought it would be nice if everyone's family had a single, large, empty picture frame or bulletin board that could easily hold photos or newspaper clippings of concern. That way the whole family could send their positive thoughts or prayers at any time of day about any or all of these visual reminders. I wouldn't build a shrine, of course, but something that is warm and inviting to keep everyone's prayers actively aiming to help in some way. It could be such an involving and thought provoking project for the whole family to contribute to maintaining a focus for their positive thoughts, concerns, passion-filled prayers and Picture Prayers.

I've gone over so many different aspects of prayer and how I go about viewing it and actually doing it. Just because I do things a certain way doesn't mean it works for everyone where it's completely satisfying. When it comes to matters of faith, I truly think that it's important to make sure that each individual adds a part of themselves into how they express their faith. I've been told by hard core Bible thumpers that there is no need for anything else except for what the Bible already says, so they shoot nothing but quotes my way as if this were their own personal voice expressing their faith in God.

For some people, this works for them, but it doesn't work for all of us. Even our pastors and priests interpret what it is they read in scripture to help congregations in their churches understand what is meant by the writings. If this is being taught even by leaders of faith, I figure it's safe to say that God understands how we need to make His teachings personal and relatable. But no single person has all of the answers, not one of us, even if we get published and preach worldwide. This then makes all of us susceptible to having to join in the adventure of finding our voices in our faith, and to hopefully have fun doing it!

Chapter 19

Analysis of a Life

At different times in my life, I admit to having thought that I was capable, in some capacity, to move mountains. It seems that most of us feel that somehow in some way, our lives are meant to be so much more than they presently are. I've heard people express how they know they can do better, and others who just keep on trying different things hoping for some kind of epiphany.

It's like this "hurry up and get noticed" race to make a name for ourselves, to leave our mark on the world for present and future generations to be inspired by what we've done. Lots of people feel they can reach their mark through having children, who carry on their respective traits and name throughout generations. Others like to look to creating wealth or fame for themselves where they can sit back and take it all in, with several onlookers wondering how they achieved their status.

When I published my first book and started up with giving talks and interviews on various television and radio shows, it changed my views on what status does in this life. What I did in writing my first book, I did it out of necessity in hopes of helping others. I personally had great fears of public speaking, where it got no better as time went on and I did more and more publicity. Yet, to some onlookers, even those who knew of my struggle to get published and give talks, they took the commoner's notion that I did what I did for status alone.

Status, even when the book was widely known to be self-published where I continued to work at a low-paying job to help keep up with my free-of-charge speaking arrangements, and fried my nerves with every interview I gave; "status craving" was pointed my way. I learned through this experience two important lessons: One is that some people don't know what it means to follow passion selflessly. Second, I observed that so many people are aiming to gain status that they even accuse others of solely going after the same thing. To some degree, it was inevitable that I did achieve a certain status for speaking out on what I did. My concerns grew, however, when I felt people gave me too much credit and sometimes asked me things I felt should only be between them and God. Status, made me feel uncomfortable, unworthy and yet, I still sought to follow my heart to help people as honestly as I could. It was a passion that drove me, and Jesus who literally promised to give me the voice to speak with.

My status here isn't what makes me feel good inside and the little I did gain, physically and mentally it wore me out to keep up on my own. I'm not silly enough to say that I'm not proud of my accomplishments, because I feel they are all God inspired, each and every one of them because I know where my heart is. I simply realized a long time ago in seeing how quickly my mother left this existence, that this life is too darn short to be all caught up in this physical world at all times.

I never thought of my physical life as being the only element that equaled "me". Even as a kid, my sister Keisha and I used to play an odd game. We used to say, "Try thinking back to the time before you were born." We'd then let our eyes roll back in our heads as we thought deeply, and I always felt a little dizzy after-wards, but there was something there. What the heck it was at the time, I couldn't say, but I could feel that there was another me before I became me.

In the United States, the average lifespan is 77 years old; 77! That's if you are lucky enough to not get killed during this mishap-filled aging process called life. In parts of Africa, the average lifespan is 37 years old. I don't know about anyone else, but even though there's a huge difference in these numbers it sure doesn't sound like a whole lot of time to me either way.

I've always liked to believe that leaving a mark on this world is more about what kind of life we can breathe into our afterlife. Life brings forth life, on more levels than in the physical world we can see and touch around us. Who can say the next life isn't part of what our physical world provides? Although, what we experience in what we see and touch, can make an impact on our souls.

When I attended Mount Mary College in Milwaukee, I was required to take a certain number of theology courses. One of the nuns, who was my instructor of one course, took the class on an interesting exercise in prayer walking along the wooded paths next to the college. Prayer walking consisted of being very purposeful in each step taken; to take the time to sense every move we made. There was no talking, no rushing, and no grouping up of students. Each person was to create their own path, pace and thoughts for all that they felt and wondered about at any time in prayer or life.

Taking the time to slow things down, students and myself, reported that they felt themselves to be more as one with the world around them. Some said it gave them time to think outside of the material things they had, and to simply observe their "being". In just one class period, many felt the outside world melt away to a less important level. Even with this feeling being embraced for a brief amount of time, I couldn't help but to wonder if the other students really knew what this meant.

Those moments of peace are allowed and needed from this hectic world. The race to attain some kind of recognizable achievement isn't meant to overshadow the quiet resolve and accomplishments of the soul. Cutting away the parts of my life that doesn't help me reach toward God, needs to happen for me so I can get my head straight on where I stand in all aspects.

Why this rat race of trying to gain a name or recognition for a contribution to the development, inspiration, or accomplishments of others, I don't feel should be measured by any one person. No matter what was done in anyone's life, there is no guarantee that it will go on to a point where it still satisfies you on the other side of life; then again, it just might. Yet, even I realize that the pages from my books might fade, and my name might not remain on anyone's lips for long; just as it should or should not be.

For all I know, a stranger can pick up something I spoke of briefly at a conference, and twenty years later they create a children's book where they cannot recall where the inspiration came from. There is no telling what me or anyone does in this lifetime that might inspire another to do great things that will encourage a generation of appreciators at any given time. Keeping score of these things is an impossible task, but not for God. He knows what we do, who heard it, who used it, where it went, how far it went, and how it helped your soul along in creating a "status" for itself in God's eyes.

After all the bright ideas, get rich quick conferences attended, bands that have been joined, countries that have been traveled to, movie ideas dreamed up, employment hopes, houses remodeled, babies born, exercises performed; and it all comes down to you talking about the idea of chocolate covered pickles to your friend who you encourage to produce them, it becomes a billion dollar company and in turn donates millions to charity each year. It's those unsuspecting things, when you selflessly give a part of yourself that unexpectedly grows into bigger things and helps so much more than imagined. These are the things I feel need to be sought out and done without even knowing what the outcome may be, but you gave a part of yourself to the thought anyhow. God knows, God watches, God keeps tabs.

It's time we go a little easier on ourselves in knowing God's on top of everything. The "I know I can do something big with my life" thoughts might already be in motion for all we know. Maybe we'll live to see what becomes of our life contributions, perhaps it was never meant for us to see what they are from this side of the mirror of life. So when I pray for something more or for something to work out better in my life, I now think that God has probably answered my prayer in the way He knows best; I just need to have faith in that!

Chapter 20

Responsibility

Something that has always come into my mind when in the face of my own spirituality or anything newly learned is that with knowledge comes responsibility. I used to hate when the phrase of "being responsible" was told to me in regard to anything while growing up or even while being a grown-up, for that matter. It was like having the "As long as you are living under my roof" speech one hears from their parents, being transformed into a Picture Prayer where the roof suddenly had my name on it!

Living my life and learning along the way goes hand-in-hand. Let's say if I were to have lightly taken the lesson on how to physically walk when I was a baby, I'd be having a hard time getting around upright today. I'm also fortunate that I am not the type to deny having learned how to walk from someone else and through my own observations. As essential as we humans physically and humanly view the act of walking, I see praying as our first non-physical acts of humanly stepping towards God. There are no other footpaths to go about reaching Him, even if He is considered to be everywhere at once. There has to be a conscious effort made, even being baptized as a baby doesn't count that baby in as having made an effort. An effort was made on their behalf, yes, but now it's their turn to take it from there.

I was truly angry at God as a child when He up and took my mother away from me. I didn't think about, "Oh, this is going to affect my little soul in the long run!" I was just simply angry, and tired of being made to sit still in His house at church to appreciate Him for all that He's done. For all that I knew or cared to understand is that He aimed to make little girls motherless and scared to move.

That's an attitude I could have chosen to keep, had I not seen at least some benefit to speak with Him so I could send a message to my mom. I now realize, if I had passed away at that young point in my life with the anger I had towards God, that I would have had to own up to it at some point. I was taught that children had some sort of Godly insurance plan where they weren't accountable for their sins up until the age of twelve, or so. But, I'm telling you now. I think God would have had to sit me down for at least a good scolding for how I viewed Him then!

There is always a choice to be made about absolutely everything in life, whether we are young, old or human. I say the word "human" because I think even animals can be seen to decide if they are bad or not, too. Just ask my dog Alien, and he'll tell you that when mama leaves I can hardly wait to sit on her bed pillow even though she's allergic to my fur. Alien knows better, but he doesn't always decide to go with what's best. Some animals even appear to prefer to bite even if there is no apparent threat, just to show they are superior or in control. Is this sort of behavior always just animal instincts, personality differences, or something else at work here? If it is just instinctual, then some people seem to have a lot more in common with animals than I first thought, and here we are supposed to be the dominant species on this planet!

Decisions are being made. Disguises are being kept and influences are being impressed upon people from positive and negative sources. God has those who are good on His side and negative forces have others at its side.

Had I not made the efforts I have to learn notions about God and trust in my heart what is right and wrong, I believe I would still be held responsible for not taking those steps. It's not like I live in a bubble where I wouldn't have even heard about God or prayer being spoken of or displayed out on an advertisement billboard off the freeway. There are avenues and pit stops all over the place to pause and consider our place in the universe of God.

Had I tossed an apple core in the street and figured it was okay to do since it was biodegradable, but I got a ticket for it; I bet I would still have to pay that darn ticket. Yeah, I had the common knowledge to know it wasn't legal to litter, but in my mind I figured, "Hey, some rabbit might just come along to find these apple bits and think it was their lucky day!" Not thinking about my having tossed it in the street where that rabbit might get run over trying to reach that apple core, causing an oncoming car to swerve to avoid the rabbit, but that's besides the point. It was all still illegal to drop anything in the street and I would have to pay for the consequence of my actions whether I knew it to be illegal or not, or caused a bunny's death.

Knowing if God would show some leniency for my ignorance in not getting to know Him or His rules, I cannot say for certain. He is the forgiving sort, but it seems there should be no excuse for not getting to know the type of standards He usually looks for in His recruits. I also have to say that I might have just contributed to there being even less of an excuse for anyone when facing Him — that is, for those of you who have read this book now.

No, I don't think this is the "tell all — know-it-all" book. I just feel it serves as an option in prayer. An option that helps encourage others to make prayer accessible at all times of day, even in a quick and complete manner. I try to be careful to not pose to be a guru or have this unattainable knowledge or access to something fully unique. God knew what I would do with what was shown to me, and how I would go about sharing it. So however Picture Prayers flows, goes or stops quickly in the mud, that's how far it was meant to go.

I can sit here and be as upbeat and anxious to share Picture Prayers as much as I want. But it's not up to me to say this is the next best thing since chocolate and have everyone agree or go along with it. So wherever my awkward and heartfelt journey to try forming picture perfect prayers goes, it will be fine with me.

Now I look at my book and wonder how in the world I was even able to ramble on about such a simple concept: To use prayer to get to know God. I don't care what it takes for anyone to feel at ease about their soul and where it stands with God, just as long as they get it there.

Get comfy, get spiritual, and get to it!

God is all knowing in what all of our needs are and what we have done in our daily lives. But even when it comes to watching our movies on DVD; it's always fun to hear the perspective of those behind the scenes on the special DVD features to see why things happened as they did during the making of the film. So I think it's best to not let God just see all of our personal performances without an explanation or tender moment behind our life's curtain before our final curtain call is made.

Life is short, unfair, reasonable, hectic, adventurous, exhausting, tickling, cold, mysterious, boring, exhilarating and harsh. But if it wasn't all of these things, it wouldn't be God's way of showing us what He can create and allow us to move those mountains He's built or have us climb over them. It's always been up to us to work with, for, against or through God, the choice is completely all of ours!

So, for all of those eyeballs I feel gracing these pages, and to all of the pondering and wandering thoughts about our soul's plight; God hears you and sees you. Own up to who you are and what He's given you, the time to be responsible for your actions and soul is **now!** Waiting until tomorrow just gives you less time and one less day to share a part of who you are with God.

Keep praying, you people I share this planet with, and I'll do the same...

Your Friend,
~Heidi

BOOKS

O is a symbol of the world, of oneness and unity. In different cultures it also means the "eye," symbolizing knowledge and insight. We aim to publish books that are accessible, constructive and that challenge accepted opinion, both that of academia and the "moral majority."

Our books are available in all good English language bookstores worldwide. If you don't see the book on the shelves ask the bookstore to order it for you, quoting the ISBN number and title. Alternatively you can order online (all major online retail sites carry our titles) or contact the distributor in the relevant country, listed on the copyright page.

See our website www.o-books.net for a full list of over 500 titles, growing by 100 a year.

And tune in to myspiritradio.com for our book review radio show, hosted by June-Elleni Laine, where you can listen to the authors discussing their books.

MySpiritRadio